THE

# GERMAN U-BOAT BASE

*at Lorient, France*

**VOLUME 1**

JUNE 1940 - JUNE 1941

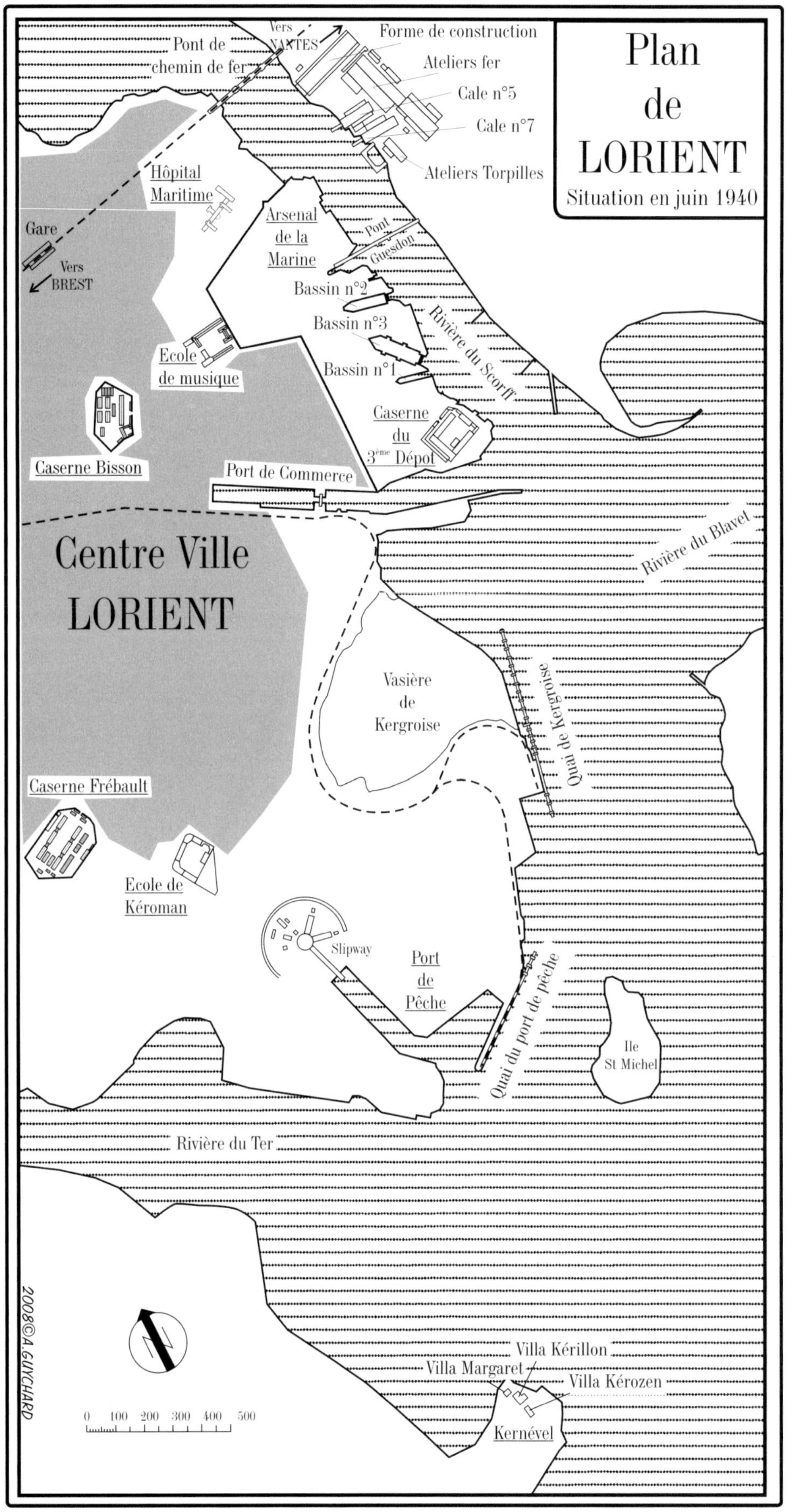
Plan
de
LORIENT
Situation en juin 1940
Vers NANTES
Forme de construction
Ateliers fer
Cale n°5
Cale n°7
Ateliers Torpilles
Pont de chemin de fer
Hôpital Maritime
Gare
Vers BREST
Arsenal de la Marine
Pont Guesdon
Bassin n°2
Bassin n°3
Bassin n°1
Rivière du Scorff
Ecole de musique
Caserne Bisson
Caserne du 3ème Dépot
Port de Commerce
Rivière du Blavet
Centre Ville
LORIENT
Vasière de Kergroise
Quai de Kergroise
Caserne Frébault
Ecole de Kéroman
Slipway
Port de Pêche
Quai du port de pêche
Ile St Michel
Rivière du Ter
Villa Kérillon
Villa Margaret
Villa Kérozen
Kernével
2008©A.GUYCHARD
0 100 200 300 400 500

JUNE 1940 - JUNE 1941

# THE GERMAN U-BOAT BASE

## *at Lorient, France*

**VOLUME 1**

LUC BRAEUER

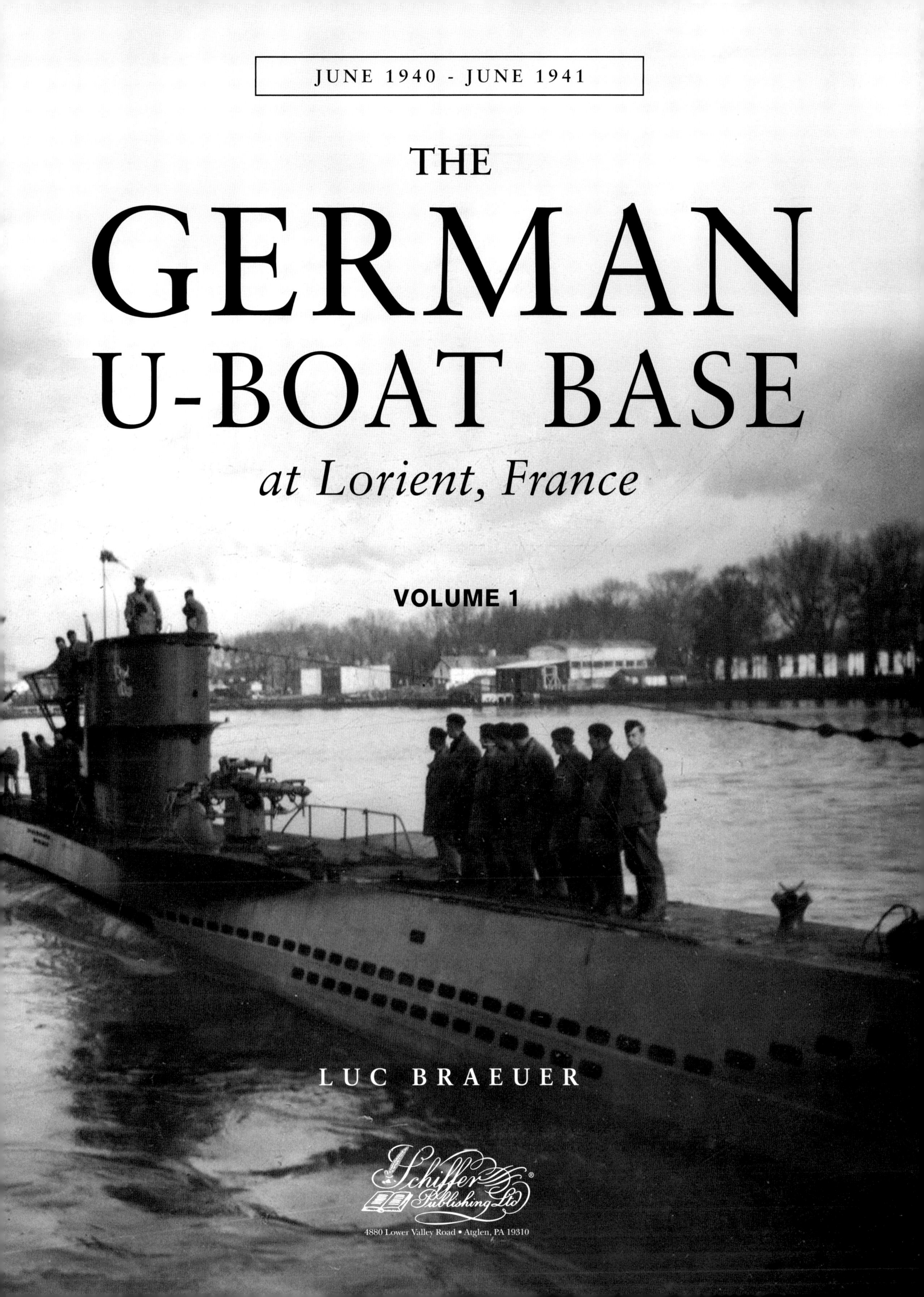

Schiffer Publishing Ltd
4880 Lower Valley Road • Atglen, PA 19310

THIS BOOK IS DEDICATED
TO THE VICTIMS OF
THE BATTLE OF THE ATLANTIC



Translated from the French
by Omicron Language Solutions, LLC.

Originally published as,
*U-Boote! Lorient: Juin 40 - Juin 41, le premier "âge d'or,"*



Library of Congress Control Number: 2015937474



Type set in Sabon & Akzidenz

ISBN: 978-0-7643-4830-3
Printed in China

Published by Schiffer Publishing, Ltd.
4880 Lower Valley Road
Atglen, PA 19310
Phone: (610) 593-1777; Fax: (610) 593-2002
E-mail: Info@schifferbooks.com

For our complete selection of fine books on this and related subjects, please visit our website at www.schifferbooks.com. You may also write for a free catalog.

This book may be purchased from the publisher. Please try your bookstore first.

We are always looking for people to write books on new and related subjects. If you have an idea for a book, please contact us at proposals@schifferbooks.com.

Schiffer Publishing's titles are available at special discounts for bulk purchases for sales promotions or premiums. Special editions, including personalized covers, corporate imprints, and excerpts can be created in large quantities for special needs. For more information, contact the publisher.

# CONTENTS

# ACKNOWLEDGMENTS

I would like to thank everyone who helped me with the creation of this book, which was a real team effort, and in particular Mr. Horst Bredow the founder and director of U-boat Archive in Cuxhaven and my two friends in Lorient Anthony Guychard and Benoît Senne, as well as Wolfgang Ockert and Bernd Siepert in Germany; Frans Beckers, Josef Charita and Walter Cloots in Belgium; Alain Chazette, Alain Destouches, Bernard Disdier, Jean Faillat, Sébastien Hervouet, Patrice Lebrun, Hervé Le Diagon, Lucien Le Pallec, Thierry Nicolo, Bernard Paich, Jean-Yves Nasse, Pierre-Marie Rousseau, Pascal Theffo, and the Archive Services BA Coblence; ECPAD Ivry; NA Washington; IWM and PRO London; SHM Vincennes; Wast Berlin; my brother Marc, my mother Monique and Alain Durrieu for their proofing and my wife Céline for her patience. ■

*Luc Braeuer*

April 2008: A souvenir from a week working in the U-boat Archives in Cuxhaven. From left to right: Anthony Guychard, Horst Bredow (archive manager), Luc Braeuer, Benoît Senne.

# PROLOGUE

In 1994, after my brother Marc and I had finished our education, we decided to dedicate our lives to the conservation and the development of the military historical heritage in France, our passion since we were very young. We have dedicated ourselves to the protection of the history of the region around St. Nazaire, a port marked by the events during the Second World War but without a museum to remind us of them. In 1997, after three years of canvassing and intensive work, we have filled a historical void by opening in Batz-sur-Mer, the *Grand Blockhaus* the museum of the St. Nazaire pocket. This museum has welcomed over 350,000 visitors in twelve years including thousands of veterans. Thanks to their accounts completed by meticulous research in the French, German, British and American military and civilian archives as well as a permanent quest for information, the second concrete result was the publication of ten historical books on the region around St. Nazaire during the Second World War, which represents more than a thousand pages published.

In September 2005, hoping to find new documentation about the sector, I went to Paris to meet with a collector who had discovered, during an inventory for an inheritance three photo albums which had belonged to a German submariner based in St. Nazaire. While going through the photos, I realized that they were albums belonging to a member of the 2nd German U-boat Flotilla's land personnel who were based permanently in Lorient from 1940 to 1945. These albums put together at the epoch, contained nearly 600 photos of the installations of U-boats, their passage in the port, their commanders and the life led by the crewmembers when ashore. Considering the considerable historical interest of these unpublished documents, I immediately decided to "dive" into the history of this port so that anyone who is interested in the history of the Battle of the Atlantic could discover it, along with the U-boats and the port in Lorient.

For three years, I worked on putting captions to all the photos and put them in a chronological

The marine belonging to the 2nd Flotilla's ground personnel who created, from 1940-1944, the three photo albums that served as a starting point for this book. *LB*

The three photo albums about U-boats in Lorient, found by the author in September 2005. *LB*

These three albums contain about 600 unpublished photos of German U-boats in Lorient. *LB*

context. This was made possible thanks to the huge amount of research carried out by two Flemish colleagues, who checked the arrival and departure dates of every U-boat passing through Lorient, in the archives of the German Navy; their lists even noted the arrival and departure time! I also owe a lot to Mr. Josef Charita's knowledge; after the war, he was responsible for military identification for the Belgian Ministry of the Interior and he very kindly helped me to put names to the faces of several commanders. Like the two young Germans Wolfgang Ockert and Bernd Siepert, he also very kindly opened his personal archives, which helped complete the background for the beginning. Several visits to the Photography Service of the French Army in Ivry, which contain an important German background "spoils of war" and the important archives of U-boats in Cuxhaven created by Mr. Horst Bredow, finished my long quest for documents. Captain Jerry Mason in Canada helped me complete my education by making available the interrogation reports of German submariners captured by the Allies after their U-boat was destroyed, documents that until then had been stored in American archives. Two collector friends in Lorient allowed me to photograph their collection of historical objects relating to U-boats in this port. Finally, two precious contacts there, who have since become close friends, guided me through the numerous vestiges marking out the passage of the German submariners throughout the region around Lorient that you will find in the folder colors.

All these documents, put together for the first time, with photos of the epoch put into chronological order month by month, completed by unpublished information, should give you a good approach to the subject of U-boats in Lorient. I haven't tried to recall all the events that occurred in the port during this period, which has been widely covered in other books; I preferred working with archives that have never been used, I have kept to the presence of the German U-boat Corps and to the numerous reactions it provoked among the Allies. ■

# INTRODUCTION

In just four years, from July 7, 1940 to September 9, 1944, the port in Lorient saw the passage of 203 different U-boats including two Japanese submarines. Twenty-seven put into port at the same time at the end of March – beginning of April 1943. These U-boats' results were impressive; for example, they had carried out the seven most efficient combat patrols achieved by U-boats during the war, sinking over 60,000 tons of Allied ships during a single patrol, which represented between ten and fourteen ships. Of the thirty-five U-boats that had sunk over 95,000 tons of enemy cargo ships during all of their patrols, thirty-three put into port in Lorient. There was a list of U-boat commanders indicating tonnage sunk; of the thirty-four commanders with over 100,000 tons to their credit, thirty-two came to Lorient. Eighty U-boat commanders passing through this port won the Knight's Cross, the highest decoration awarded during combat at the epoch. The port in Lorient was incontestably the most important German U-boat base during the Second World War.

From Lorient, most of U-boats left to hunt in the Atlantic right to the American coast, from the Brazilian waters to the St. Laurent River in Canada. Others found themselves trapped in the Mediterranean while some crossed the Indian Ocean and reached the Far East. Several carried out special patrols disembarking secret agents in Ireland, on the African or U.S. coasts. Most of them were lost in combat with their entire crews, sometimes in the Bay of Biscay just after leaving Lorient. One of the last to call in this port, U-853, was sunk on May 6, 1945, just off New York, while U-530 only surrendered when it arrived off Argentina on July 10, 1945!

In this first volume, covering the period from June 1940 to June 1941, you will discover the evacuation of the port by the French Navy and their fight for the honor. It details the installation of the German Navy in Lorient and the first year of U-boat presence in this port, as well as the important stages of the Battle of the Atlantic in which they participated. The U-boats that put into Lorient were presented on monthly charts according to their type, their flotilla, their commander and the date they were put into service. You will see the exact dates of their stay in the port and their fate when they left for the last time. You will discover the life lived by the crewmembers on shore while their U-boats were being repaired and the naval and aerial actions carried out by the British on the port in Lorient. This first book will be followed next year by a second tome covering the period of July 1941 to July 1942, which will discuss the attacks on the American coast, while two other tomes will cover later years and patrols in remote oceans, the fate of U-boats faced with the landing in Normandy and finally their final departure from Lorient. ■

# JUNE 1940, THE WAR REACHES LORIENT

## *The French Navy Evacuates the Port and Fights to Keep the Arsenal*

Having marched into Paris on June 14, the German troops arrived in Rennes three days later, a few hours after the radio diffusion of Field-Marshal Pétain announcing that armistice negotiations were underway. On this same day, June 17, two British emissaries arrived in Lorient, they had come to organize the departure for England of about twenty cargo ships, principally Norwegian and Dutch; as from the following day these ships came to the aid of the British Merchant Navy. In Lorient, in the first hours of June 18, German Heinkel 111 bombers from the KG 4 Combat Squadron dropped magnetic mines in the west of the English Channel; the next day the trawler "La Tanche" ran into one after leaving Lorient and about 190 people on board were killed. Meanwhile, in London General DeGaulle made his famous speech and in Lorient Squadron Rear-Admiral Hervé de Penfentenyo de Kervereguin, commander of the 5th Région Maritime began the evacuation of all military buildings and the destruction of anything which couldn't be carried away. He organized the departure of about fifty warships and the ex-banana-ship "Victor Schoelcher," turned into an auxiliary cruiser and was full of gold from Belgian and Polish banks! He had most of the personnel from military buildings in the town evacuated by sea, notably the students in the apprentice mechanics' school, the Fusiliers Marins and the radio operators. The arsenal's port installations were destroyed and the ten fuel-oil tanks in Priatec containing 95,000 tons of fuel-oil were set on fire; the explosion of one of them killed twenty-five civilians in the nearby town of Cosquer on June 25; the fire continued burning until July 25.

During the night of June 18/19, Admiral Le Luc, born in Lorient, Chief of Admiral Darlan's General Staff and Commander-in-Chief of the French Navy, ordered Rear-Admiral de Penfentenyo by telephone: "Defend Lorient at all cost!" This order was justified by the necessity of fighting as a matter of principle so that the Germans wouldn't consider the arsenal as "spoils of war." However, the means of defense had been sabotaged and there weren't a lot of people left in the empty port where the installations had also been destroyed. Besides, this order was contradictory to the directive from the Ministry of the Interior of the same day, which had announced that towns of more than 20,000 habitants were to be considered "open cities." To execute the first order without contradicting the second, on June 19, Rear-Admiral de Penfentenyo set up a roadblock on the road to Quimper, about ten kilometers from the town, at a locality called "Les Cinq chemins" in Guidel. On June 21 at 9:15, the Germans arriving in front of the roadblock were stopped, and a confrontation with the French lasted over three hours. Six Germans were killed and six French soldiers, but their honor was saved.

The population of Lorient was kept informed of German command instructions by the local newspaper "Le nouvelliste du Morbihan" which came out between four and five o'clock, even before the German troops arrived in town! The Occupants' directives, transmitted at two o'clock to the daily paper, were notably that the public services should continue working and that henceforth alcohol was prohibited in the cafés ... except wine, cider and beer! All members of the French military were to gather at six o'clock in Keryado. Circulation would be prohibited in town after ten o'clock except for emergency services.

That day, June 21, 1940 at 18:00, a column of German troops entered Lorient and marched to the Maritime Prefecture where Admiral de Penfentenyo was waiting. He said to the German officer: "I have nothing to give you. Everything that can fly has flown; everything that can float has sailed away. Even the torpedo-ship Bouclier, amputated in the front end, has been towed away by the rear end; they are safe in England. All our supplies have been destroyed. Our dry docks are unusable. Our banks are empty. I have burnt all our currency so that you can't get your hands on it. The keys of Lorient, the pure symbol of which the Navy named me keeper, have been put in a safe place. Finally, I have removed my sword to avoid having to surrender it to you." On the subject of the sword, the German officer replied: "I regret that, Admiral, because it would have been my duty to restore it to you immediately!" Around 6,000 French soldiers and marines were taken prisoner and sent to Pont-Scorff. The French/German Armistice was signed the next day in Compiegne. ■

Hervé de Penfentenyo de Kervereguin, Squadron Vice-Admiral, commander of the 5th Maritime Region, is in charge of evacuation operations in Lorient Port on June 18, 1940. His authority extended from the *Pointe de la Torche* coast to the coast of the Spanish border. *DR*

About fifty warships leave Lorient Port on June 18, 1940; the old sloop *"Enseigne Hénri,"* launched in 1918, was scuttled where it lay at anchor. Raised by the Germans, it would later be used as a berthing platform for U-boats. The old sloops "*Audacieuse*" and "*Surveillant*" and the barge "*Isère,*" which are already being used as berthing platforms, stayed intact on the Scorff too; they survived the tide of flames that spread out following the burning of the fuel barrels in Priatec. *DR*

June 21 at 09:30: the French, positioned in Cinq Chemins in Guidel since the previous evening, open fire on the German convoy which has just arrived in Quimperlé. The car of the Chief of the 7th Company of the *Maschinen Gewehr Bataillon 1* is hit. *LB*

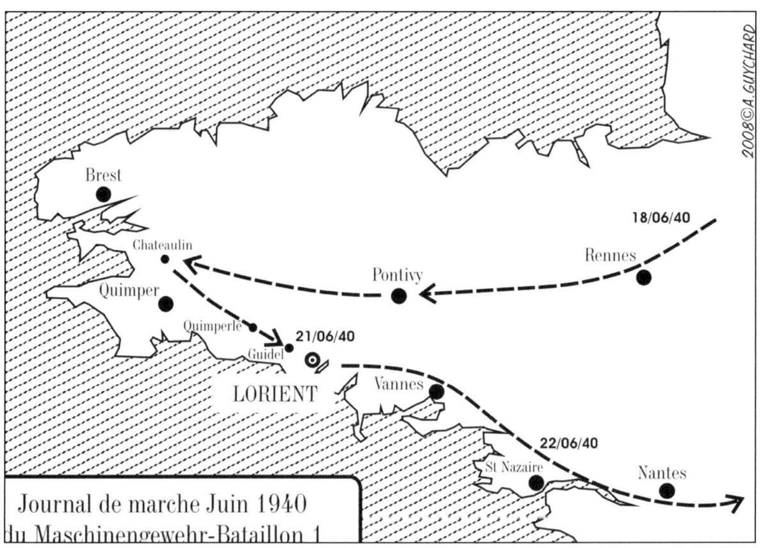

Two old cruisers, launched before 1918, have been left intact in Lorient Port. On the left: the armored cruiser *"Condé,"* launched in 1904, which once served as barracks for the *Fusiliers Marins* in Lorient from 1931 to 1933, the year it was taken out of service. It was then used as a berthing platform in front of the Péristyle barracks until 1940; the following year the Germans towed it to Royan, where it was used as a target. On the right: in front of the *Pointe de l'Espérance*, the light cruiser *Strasbourg*, which the Germans will use as an anti-aircraft post in the harbor; this was the former *Regensburg*, a German ship launched in 1914 and given to France in 1920 as war reparations; when the Germans arrived, it was berthed alongside the rough lumber hangar; Hans Ibekken, the Chief of the 2nd U-boat Flotilla from October 1937 to September 1939, served aboard this ship as a cadet in November 1919! On the right: the TSF pylons belonging to the radio station in Pen Mané. *LB*

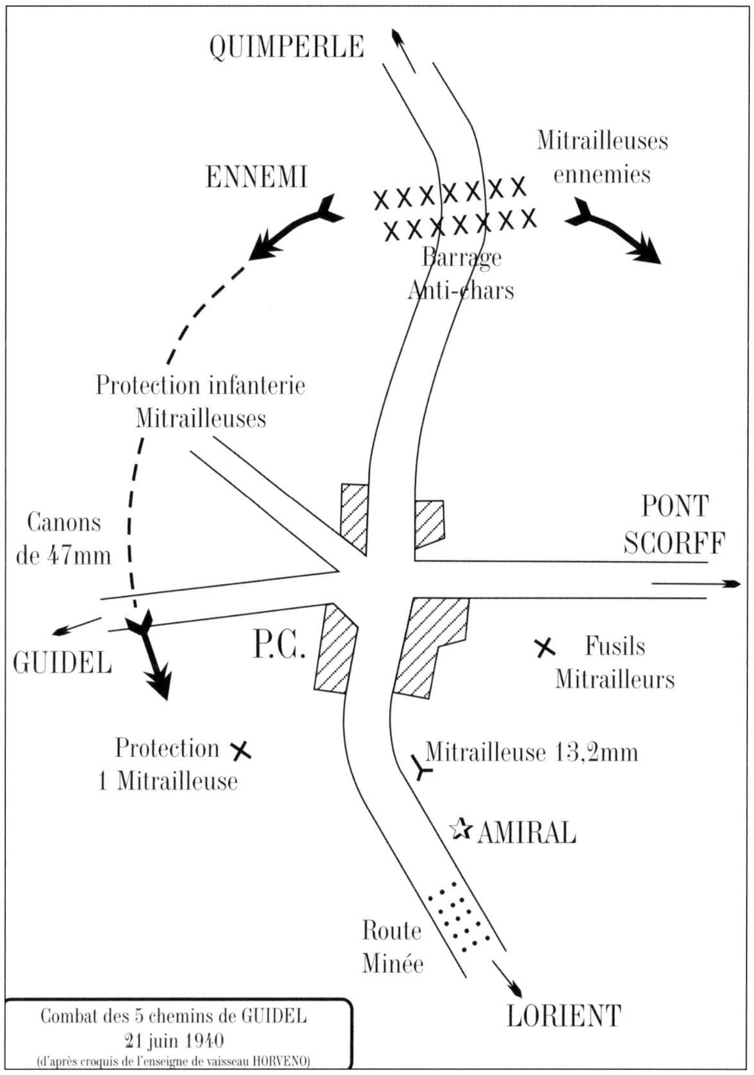

In the morning of June 21, 1940, the German soldiers of the *7./M.G.-Bat. 1*, have taken up position in the heights of Cinq Chemins in Guidel, with a *Pak* 3.7cm anti-tank gun. They immediately aim for the French defense position. The series of photos from June 21-22, 1940, comes directly from the personal album of a soldier of *M.G.-Bat. 1. LB*

A quadruple 13.2mm anti-aircraft machine gun belonging to the French Navy has been brought to Port-Louis in Cinq Chemins on the evening of June 20. To man it are twenty-two marines once part of the DCA Battery in Kerner, under the command of Ensign Horveno. The machine gun has been placed alongside the road, after the crossroads that winds down to Lorient. We can also see the sandbags brought in trucks from Lorient at around 21:00. *LB*

The 11th Brigade of Motorized Protection (*11. Schützen Brigade mot.*), whose insignia is a ghost with a glaive in its hand, arrives in Lorient on June 21, 1940. *LB*

The *11. Schützen Brigade*, commanded by *Oberst* Günther Angern, has *Panzer II* and *III* tanks, which have just been used in the entire French campaign. This unit finished its route in the region around St. Nazaire and La Baule on June 23. *LB*

The envoys chat at Cinq Chemins in Guidel. We can see, just behind the marine in white uniform, is an officer of the French Navy surrounded by German soldiers. *LB*

A Red Cross truck takes French marines to the arsenal. On the right: sandbags set up as a barricade. *LB*

After fighting that lasted about three hours, and cost the lives of six French fighters and six German soldiers, the time for parley has arrived. The French envoys talk with the German soldiers in front of the *café-tabac* in Cinq Chemins. It was from here that the Germans had telephoned the Maritime Prefecture to warn them that their troops were advancing towards Lorient and were about 10km away, following the French prisoners. *LB*

The provisional tombs of the six German soldiers from the 7th *MG-Bat 1* Company, killed on June 21 during the fighting in Cinq Chemins. *LB*

A commemorative plaque, unveiled on May 15, 1966, with the names of the six French soldiers killed in the fighting in Cinq Chemins; most of them from the Colonial Artillery. *LB*

On June 21, around 18:00, the German soldiers enter Lorient from the north; they take *rue Paul Guieysse* to reach the Maritime Prefecture. *LB*

Watched by members of the French Navy, who are gathered in front of the Maritime Prefecture, following directives from the Germans in the "*Le Nouvelliste du Morbihan*" newspaper, the *MG-Bat. 1* motorcyclists arrive one after the other to park on the arsenal's *Place d'Armes. LB*

The French marines are waiting for the Germans to decide what to do with them, when a German motorcyclist passes on the right. We can see three officers leaning over the door of Gabriel Pavilion with the words *"Secteur de Défense"* written over it; the 5th Maritime Region was divided in two: the defense sector in Lorient and the Rochefort defense sector. *LB*

Taken prisoner, French marines gather in front of the prefecture and receive the order to go to Pont-Scorff, where about 6,000 men are interned. *LB*

The column of French marines on *Cours Chazelles* watched by the powerless civilians, who hope they will return quickly. *LB*

On the order of Admiral Darlan, Commander-in-Chief of the French Navy, the military arsenal's French personnel hadn't been evacuated in order to keep the 4,000 laborers' employed. The Germans didn't send the officers of the assimilated corps to the prison camp in the hopes of putting them into service; therefore, they stayed where they were. *LB*

The German vehicles belonging to *MG-Bat. 1,* commanded by *Oberstleutnant* André, are parked on the *Place d'Armes*, in front of the Gabriel Pavilions bandstand. A German flag has been raised on top of the *Tour de la Découverte* that dominates the arsenal. On the back of the car parked on the right, we can identify its unit: *MG-Bat. 1. LB*

The Germans continue their progression through the town; they take possession of *Quartier Frébault*, which had been used by the French Colonial Artillery. In the background enormous clouds of smoke caused by the destruction of the Navy's fuel dumps. *LB*

Life goes on: Place Alsace-Lorraine under the new curfew and traffic restrictions imposed by the occupiers. Note the smoke column caused by the burning of the oil reserves at the arsenal. *LB*

The "*Camp de Genêts*" (Camp Broom-bush) was built in Hennebont to house the 1,400 German laborers working on naval constructions; it is relatively far from the places targeted by Allied bombardments. *LB*

*Place des Princes* in Pont-Scorff: *NSKK-Truppführer* Schuh of the *Haupttransportkolonne 8* (Main Transport Column), transferred to the *Todt Organization* in Lorient, is in charge of transporting the material for the construction of huts in the laborers' camp, called "Kermoisan." *LB*

# The German Army Settles in Lorient

On June 23, *Konteradmiral* Karl Dönitz, commander of the German U-boat Corps, inspected the port in Lorient. Three days later, the decision was made to make it the first fortifications for U-boats in France. On June 24, Gabriel Hotel's pavilion, home of the former French Maritime Prefecture, became the offices of a German Port Commander, *Korvettenkapitän* Friedrich Badermann. The *Hafenkommandantur* (Harbor Commander's Office) that he ran organized the traffic inside the port, ensured the protection of the port's installations such as the locks and the cranes, made sure the lighthouse's lamp was operational, ensure the services of the port pilot and the displacement of ships in the port using requisitioned tugs. His service was also in charge of controlling the French fishing boats. However, the Port Commander didn't intervene in operations in the arsenal zone which housed U-boats. Commanded by Engineer *Korvettenkapitän* Waldemar Seidel, a new service of deposit and supply was specially created for the U-boats. It was made up of specialized workers from the arsenal in Wilhelmshaven who arrived by train directly from Germany. This train, prepared in advance in Wilhelmshaven on Dönitz's orders, also carried twenty-four torpedoes, air compressors and supplies materiel. Under the responsibility of the director of the Torpedo Department in Wilhelmshaven shipyard, *Kapitän-zur-See* Clamor von Trotha, the train was sent to Paris on June 23 and from there to the port. At the beginning the German workers from the shipyards were lodged near the arsenal in the former French barracks. Later a place in the country near Hennebont was specially built for them: Camp *des Genêts*. The 1,400 workers who were lodged there had heated hut sanitary facilities, a canteen and a modern infirmary as well as a large room used as a theatre or cinema; in the event of air raids, they could shelter in the 1,200 meter stone quarries situated below the camp.

The town came under German occupation on June 24. The next day, an order in the press prohibited listening to English radio. On June 28, another order was given for the surrender of all firearms, except for hunting rifles. The same day, on the order of the Prefect, circulation (cars and motorbikes) would be subjected from then on to prior authorization from the German authorities. On July 1, a curfew from 23:00 to 06:00 was imposed and all newspapers and other publications were subject to German censorship.

The barracks in the town, which had remained empty after the departure of the French Army, were quickly filled with marines, workers and German drivers. The Péristyle barracks was renamed *Saltzwedel Kaserne*, the given name of the 2nd U-boat Flotilla a part of which had been assigned to the port. This name was in homage to a former German U-boat commander in World War I, Reinhold Saltzwedel, holder of the War Merit Cross, who had sunk 111 ships before being killed on December 2, 1917 when his U-boat ran into a mine. Along with the nearby apprentice mechanics' barracks, it was used by a part of the 2nd Flotilla's General Staff and land personnel as well as by U-boats' crewmembers returning from patrols. Not all the flotilla's personnel came to Lorient immediately because, until June 1941, the 2nd Flotilla was divided between Lorient and Wilhelmshaven, its home port in Germany. The first two officers responsible for the installation until September 1940, sent from Germany on June 23, came directly from Dönitz's General Staff: *Kapitän-sur-See* Helmut Brümmer-Patzig seconded by Engineer *Kapitänleutnant* Hans Looschen. They were replaced at the beginning of July by the Chief of the 2nd Flotilla, *Korvettenkapitän* Heinz Fischer, charged with directing the entire installation operation of the unit in Lorient. Contrary to other units of the Kriegsmarine, the U-boat flotillas' chiefs didn't decide the tactical use of their U-boats, Dönitz and his General Staff took care of it. They were only there to organize welcome receptions for the U-boats and their crewmembers, manage administration and logistical problems and ensure a link with the shipyards. This latter task was directly ensured by *Kapitänleutnant (Ing.)* Karl Scheel, Chief Engineer of the 2nd Flotilla, nick-named "Papa Scheel" by the crewmembers. *Korvettenkapitän* Hugo Baehr, 1st Administration Officer of the flotilla, was in liaison with the different authorities in place to solve the different administrative duties such as the installation of the kitchens, storing supplies and setting up different clothing workshops (tailors, cobblers, etc.) Three bunkers for the, two of which were huge and on two storeys, were built later by the *Todt Organization* in the middle of the barracks and on the quay along the Scorff to protect the flotillas' land personnel and the crewmembers returning from patrols. To entertain the crews, a large school near Kéroman, which had a lot of reception rooms and even a theater, was requisitioned and turned into a submariners' hostel – U-boats-*Heim*. The construction of this new school had been almost finished when the Germans arrived and hadn't even opened its doors to students! In Hennebont, Château Kerlois was requisitioned to house the Fortifications Company, charged with defending the arsenal from fire and air attacks, and also to act as an Honor Guard during ceremonies; the future bandstand of the 2nd Flotilla, coming from an old disarmed cruiser, was also installed. Finally, the principal clothing depot was to be found in the same town.

The former *Frébault* district that had been used by the French Colonial Infantry was re-named *Seydlitz Kaserne*. It housed the German Army soldiers based in Lorient and the NSKK truck drivers who took care of transporting equipment. Several wooden barracks were built on the nearby location of a former PTA, and were used for lodging the first several hundred Germans who worked for the *Todt Organization* constructing concrete buildings. To protect them and their equipment, they soon had about twenty bunkers built nearby. In 1941, faced with the considerable increase in the number of workers in the U-boat bases and on the Atlantic Wall, over a dozen other camps were built. They were set up in the countryside around Lorient, far from air raids. The largest, destined to lodge about 1,500 workers, was in Hennebont; opened in March 1941, it was nicknamed *Camp Franco* because large numbers of Spanish workers were housed there. The *Todt Organization's* General Staff *for* the Lorient sector, *Oberbauleitung* Mitte, requisitioned the Young Women's College buildings. The 2nd Company of the *14th Marine-Kraftfahr-Abteilung*, transport service of the *Kriegsmarine*, settled in the Bisson barracks renamed *Hindenburg Kaserne*. The new and modern French Maritime Hospital, situated in the extension of the arsenal, was also requisitioned by the Kriegsmarine and renamed *Marine-Lazarett-Lorient*. ■

The huts in the Kermoisan laborers' camp in Pont-Scorff were built by July 1940. *LB*

The Germans requisition French shells abandoned in the arsenal. We can see the back of the central building that will house the future municipal museum in Lorient and which was an annex of the Town Hall in 1940. This collection of buildings will be requisitioned to house the 2nd U-boat Flotilla's ground personnel.

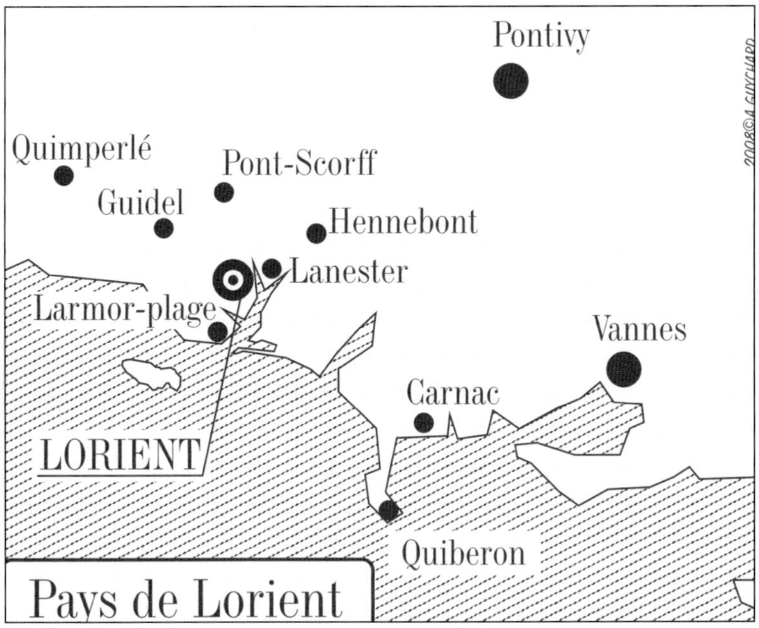
Pontivy
Quimperlé
Pont-Scorff
Guidel
Hennebont
Lanester
Larmor-plage
Vannes
Carnac
LORIENT
Quiberon
Pays de Lorient

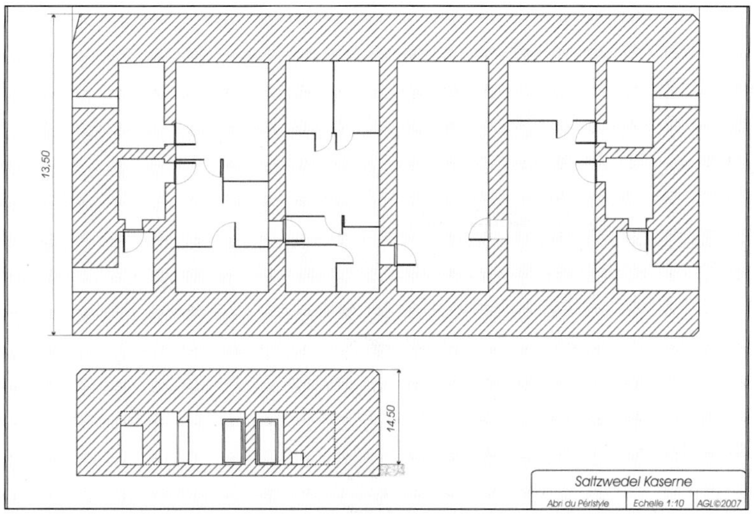
13,50
14,50
Saltzwedel Kaserne
Abri du Péristyle
Echelle 1:10
AGL©2007

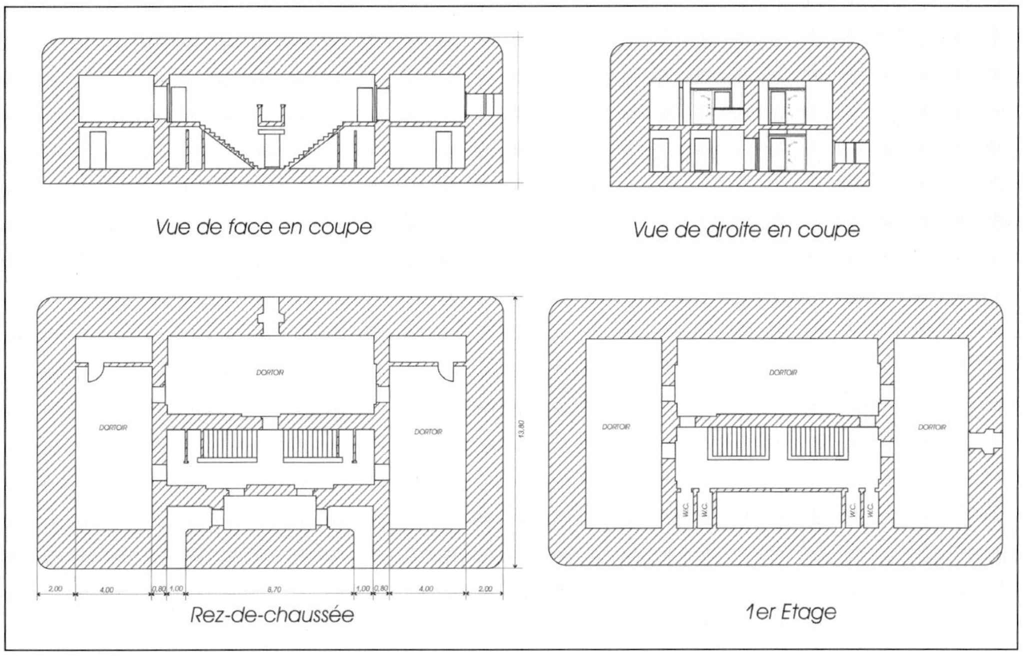
Vue de face en coupe
Vue de droite en coupe
DORTOIR
13,80
2,00
4,00
0,80
1,00
8,70
1,00
0,80
4,00
2,00
Rez-de-chaussée
W.C.
1er Etage

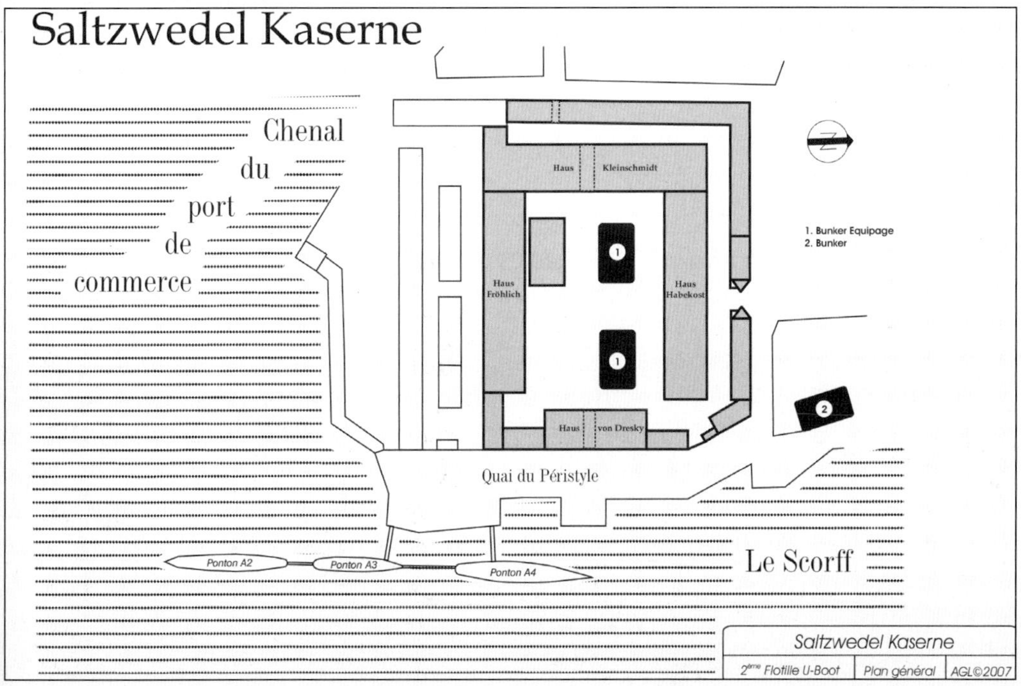
Saltzwedel Kaserne
Chenal du port de commerce
Haus Kleinschmidt
Haus Fröhlich
Haus Habekost
Haus von Dresky
1. Bunker Equipage
2. Bunker
Quai du Péristyle
Le Scorff
Ponton A2
Ponton A3
Ponton A4
Saltzwedel Kaserne
2ème Flotille U-Boot
Plan général
AGL©2007

The doors to the arsenal are guarded by both the German Navy and the French police. A bi-lingual sign instructs laborers to dismount their bicycles to have their passes controlled. *LB*

The German war flag floats over the Péristyle barracks, re-named *"Saltzwedel Kaserne,"* the given name of the 2nd U-boat Flotilla, in memory of World War I U-boat Commander Reinhold Saltzwedel. *LB*

A large room in the barracks is turned into a cafe. Large paintings decorate the walls and a maxim is framed over the door. *LB*

In another room used as a canteen, an artist has painted the evolution of the U-boat Corps from its origins in 1472 to the Second World War. The blazon of Lorient has been painted in the center. *LB*

Inscriptions painted on the barracks' doors indicate where the material for the naval construction should be stored. On the left: the marine who will create the three photo albums discovered by the author in 2005. *LB*

This photo taken from the top of the *Tour de la Découverte*, gives a view of the *Saltzwedel Kaserne*; on the left in the courtyard is part of the concrete roof of the personnel's shelter. *LB*

The two big, two-story bunkers, built in the center of the barracks' courtyard, have room for the Flotilla's ground personnel and its crews in the event of an air raid. *LB*

A third bunker for personnel was built by the *Todt Organization* on the quay, in front of the sail-loft and the *Cours aux Ancres*, which are used by the Service of Naval Construction – *Ressort IIII Schiffbau* – of the German Naval war shipbuilding. *BA*

The school in Kéroman, only a few hundred meters from the future U-boat shelter building site, has been turned into a submariners' home. A large eagle is being installed on the wall. *LB*

This large school, which even has a big theater, had just been finished when the Germans arrived and had not opened its doors to students. *LB*

A bar is set up in the school. It is decorated with draperies with seascapes painted on them. *LB*

A living room for submariners. *UBA*

Chateau Kerlois is turned into a hostel for the fortifications company in charge of firefighting in the arsenal and to form honor guards during ceremonies. *LB*

Chateau Kerlois in Hennebont, used by the *Pères Blancs* (White Fathers) for their seminaries is requisitioned by the German Navy and re-named *Wilhelm Bauer Kaserne*, as homage to the German engineer, born in 1822, who had invented several models of hand-operated submarines. *UBA*

A sports field next to Chateau Kerlois gives the Honor Company a place to rehearse maneuvers during ceremonies. *LB*

A large wooden barrack is set up behind the two wings of the two Maritime Prefecture's pavilions, over a large bunker for the General Staff. This barrack is a hostel/canteen for Navy Officers of the 2nd Flotilla. *LB*

Stocks of French rifles are taken from a building in the *Frébault* district. These firearms will probably be distributed to the auxiliary units of the Army, such as the *Todt Organization. LB*

*Frébault* district, former HQ of the French Colonial Artillery, is occupied by the Army soldiers of *MG-Bat. 1. LB*

The *MG-Bat 1* soldiers maneuver in a courtyard in the *Frébault* district. After the May-June 1940 campaign, barracks life reasserts itself. *LB*

June 22, 1940: A German Henschel 126 reconnaissance plane has had to make an emergency landing in Lorient; it landed next to the *Frébault* district, near the rifle range. *LB*

Badly damaged during its emergency landing, the Henschel 126 is towed by a tanker truck. *LB*

The drivers of the *NSKK-Transportkolonne 8* also settled into a building in the *Frébault* district at the end of June 1940. They are there to give the *Todt Organization* help with logistics. *LB*

Several members of the *NSKK-Transportkolonne 8* are in charge of removing the charred remains of the barrels in the oil dump situated along the fuel tankers' wharf on the left bank on the Lanester side; they were sabotaged by the French Navy in 1940. On the right: *Truppführer* Schuh; on the left: a driver dressed in a British jacket that the British Expeditionary Force in France had abandoned along with a lot of others in a depot in Lorient. Like the *Todt Organization*, the *NSKK* Transport Unit had brown uniforms, similar to those worn by the Allies. *LB*

The laborers start clearing away the charred barrels in the oil dump; the truck has the inscriptions *Todt Organization* and *Wehrmacht* on it. *LB*

Work on concreting the bunkers, notably at Kernével, where the Command of the U-boat Corps' HQ will be, started in the summer of 1940. *LB*

The large maritime hospital in Lorient, situated in continuation of the arsenal, is requisitioned by the *Kriegsmarine.* This is where the submariners have their obligatory medical checkup before each new patrol. On the left we can see a small sign reading "*Wache*" indicating the way to the guardroom. *Alain Chazette*

View of *Marine-Lazarett* taken from the school of music. This hospital is where the submariners have their obligatory medical checkup before each new patrol. *LB*

German members of the *Kriegsmarinewerft Lorient* (War Naval Shipyard, Lorient) in front of an arsenal building, sent from Wilhelmshaven, are wearing work uniforms without insignia on them and the regulation German Navy garrison cap. *LB*

These workers, who are posing in front of the railings of the Lorient arsenal's *Place d'Armes* are wearing grayish-green uniforms, the same model as the German Coastal Navy, but their jackets do not have the national insignia and shoulder boards. They are also wearing seized French belts. *LB*

The workers at *KMW Lorient* use a motorboat to visit the arsenal. *LB*

A break outside the workshop during the summer of 1940. *LB*

Daily work routine of the German workers in a former French arsenal workshop. *LB*

These workers from *KMW* on the winter garden rails on a U-boat maneuvering to enter a dock. On their garrison caps they still have the insignia of the Wilhelmshaven's shipyard, where they worked before. It was the only arsenal the Germans had kept after World War I. *LB*

Relaxing in front of a wooden barrack built for the workers of the naval shipyards; this one is used by the Petty Officers. *LB*

These members of *KMW Lorient*, who have been given a bottle, pose in front of the bandstand on the *Place d'Armes*, opposite Gabriel Hotel's pavilions. Some of them seem to be very young; the fourth from the left still hasn't removed the orange and white collartabs of the Coastal Navy. *LB*

Two comrades from *KMW Lorient* in regulation uniform showing black collar tabs with metal anchors attached to them. *LB*

During their free time, notably in the evening in their dormitory, they play cards. *LB*

A U-boat commander with his white cap. *LB*

The members of *KMW Lorient* have decorated their dormitory in the arsenal in April 1941 with faces painted above their wardrobes. *LB*

Another woman, whose portrait is signed by the star and dated April 8, 1941. *LB*

They discover local products … the famous Brittany lobster! *LB*

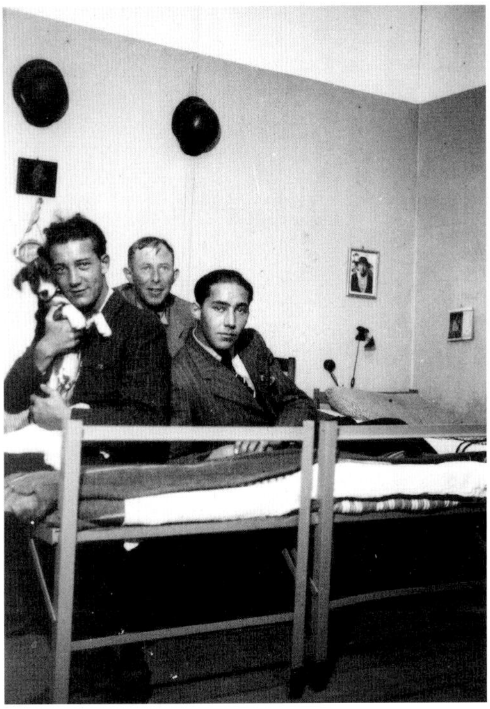

They wear civilian dress to visit the town on Sundays. *LB*

They stop by a café in the town center. *LB*

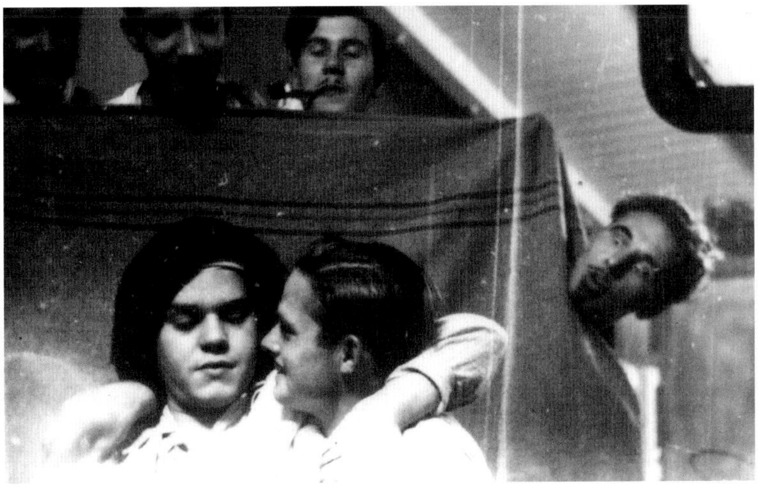

They wear costumes and go on the stage to amuse themselves. *LB*

Inside the café. *LB*

During a day off, these German workers from the naval shipyards stroll in Lorient's town center in front of a Peugeot dealership. Those on the left have added a personal touch to their uniforms by sewing on black collar tabs with metal anchors fixed to them. *LB*

Even though these members of *KMW Lorient* are wearing work overalls, they are still wearing their shirts and ties. The dock's *Cours des Quais. LB*

Billiards in the café. *LB*

These men are taking a break on a public bench in the *Quai des Indes*, near the loading dock for Port-Louis. *LB*

The man on the right, in a civilian suit and an open shirt, looks like a tourist on the seaside. They are probably in front of a casino on Port-Louis beach. *LB*

Summer 1940: It's time for swimming trunks, towel, and sunglasses on the rocks in front of Port-Louis. *LB*

Another photo-souvenir collector; this time it's a *KMW Lorient* worker. *LB*

This photo of members of *KMW Lorient* in the crow's-nest of the armored cruiser *Condé* on the Scorff; taken from one of the two photo albums being filled by the photo collector. *LB*

Around July 20, 1940, the submariners of U-52 chat before their departure planned for July 27. In the background: U-58 IIC-type U-boat and the armored cruiser *Condé*. *UBA*

A young member of *KMW* on guard duty in a rather humoristic manner … in swimming trunks. *LB*

The same man in Lorient's town center, on *Place Aristide Briand*, in his civilian suit on Sunday. *LB*

Once again – on the Port-Louis beach with a friend. *LB*

Photo souvenir of Port-Louis during the summer of 1941. *LB*

# JULY - DECEMBER 1940, "HAPPY DAYS" FOR U-BOATS IN LORIENT

## *How Lorient Changed the Situation of the German U-boats*

On May 24, 1940, Hitler lifted all restrictions in the U-boat war. He declared a total blockade of the British coast on August 17, which meant that even ships belonging to neutral countries found in the sector were liable to be sunk on sight. Therefore, until the campaign in Norway, the British didn't seem to be too threatened by the German U-boat Corps, whose actions proved to be catastrophic due to defective magnetic torpedoes, and then the situation changed. Until the end of the year U-boats lived what their commanders called "the Happy Days" or the "First Golden Age," to such a point that Commander Kretschmer of U-99 declared: "*We were like school children at Christmas!*"

Indeed, the British situation deteriorated after the campaign in France: the Royal Navy not only had to send escort ships to the Mediterranean to protect its transport ships after Italy entered the war on June 10, 1940 but also had to maintain their forces against an eventual German attack on Britain. After the French-German Armistice on June 22, it had to spread out its thin escort ships to protect its convoys whose defense until then had been ensured by the French Navy. So while the British means of defense weren't strong, with only 200 escort ships available, the potential U-boat targets were numerous: when it entered the War, the British owned a merchant fleet of about 9,500 ships totaling twenty-one million tons. When Germany invaded Norway and Holland, their Merchant Navies joined forces with the British fleet, so they could count on about 3,500 new ships totaling 7.8 million tons, which increased the dispersal of the escort ships. With the huge British merchant fleet hardly touched, there were over 12,000 cargo ships which became potential targets for the Axis. Also, at that time, there were few warships or planes to protect them. With U-boats sailing out of Lorient, the convoy traffic

A return route was painted on the two doors of a *MG-Bat 1* car leaving Lorient for its garrison town of Euskirchen in mid-July 1940. The following month this battalion will be integrated into the *16th Panzer Division,* which will be wiped out in Stalingrad at the beginning of 1943. It was replaced in Lorient by soldiers of the 211th Infantry Division. *LB*

Settling in Paris on September 1, 1940, the staff of *Konteradmiral* Karl Dönitz, commander of the U-boat Corps, are closer to the Atlantic. As he will say to his chief-of-staff in the operations department, *Korvettenkapitän* Godt, on the left in front of the chart, Dönitz thinks that thanks to the capture of French ports the victory against England is now possible. He will start to set up wolf-pack attack tactics that he had tested before the war. *Bernd Siepert* arriving from the South of Ireland was directly threatened; these convoys were rerouted north of Scotland, which increased the density of merchant ships in the Western Approaches zone, the area of sea that stretched from the west of the British Isles to the fifteenth meridian west.

On the other hand, U-boats' situation improved. With the other bases installed in the ports of Occupied Norway, the German U-boats could attack the maritime traffic heading to the British Isles from the north and the south at the same time. During the first four months, the targets were so numerous and the attacks took place so close to the British coast, between the tenth and the fifteenth meridian, that the attacker hardly had time to call other U-boats to the area; the war was a personal matter for each of them. Their new base in Lorient allowed them to save fuel and time to reach their zone of operation in the Atlantic. The economy of a week of time-out per sortie meant that the number of U-boats present in the zones of operation increased by 25%. It was thanks to these advantages that in September Dönitz put his wolfpack tactics into use with the first big successes in October: several U-boats attacked the convoys together like a pack of wolves, preferably on the surface during the night, which allowed them to counter the *Asdic*; the Allies' locating system only worked on U-boats below the surface. Sometimes they even slipped into the center of a convoy to panic and destabilize the escort ships. This was also possible thanks to the installation of a Command Post in Paris in September 1940 and then in Lorient two month later; in getting closer to the theatre of operations, the Command of U-boat Operations improved its radio liaisons and therefore the coordination of its forces against the convoys. As they didn't have to return to Germany, the U-boats avoided the North Sea where British planes and destroyers patrolled. In addition, their commanders began to get battle experience and their torpedo problems had been momentarily resolved by only using explosion-on-contact models. In November, U-boats widened their hunting grounds towards the west beyond the fifteenth meridian, where the merchant ships had no escorts or plane protection and once they were detected, other chasers had time to reach the convoys. Lastly, new, more effective VIIC-type U-boats were put into service in the second half of 1940. All these reasons explain the successes that U-boats registered until the end of the year, and mainly those out of Lorient. ■

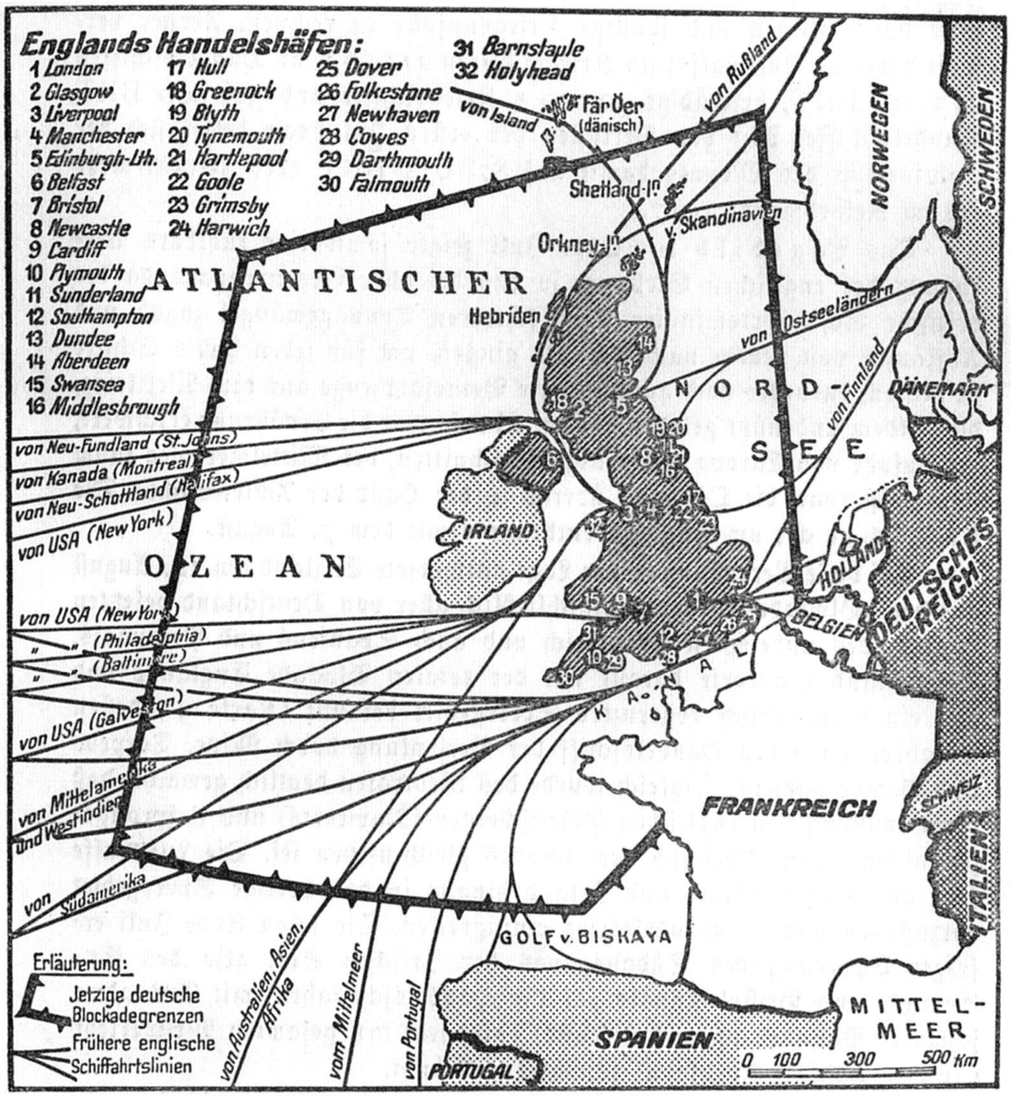


Chart delimiting the German blockade zone around the British Isles from August 17, 1940; even neutral countries' ships risked being sunk in this sector. *LB*

In the Scorff, the armored cruiser *Condé* will be used as a deposit ship for the U-boat Flotilla during their transfer to Lorient. On the left the high-speed motorboat-minesweeper belonging to the *2nd Räumboots-flotilla*, used for clearing magnetic mines from Lorient Port; its insignia is a three-pronged fork. *LB*

On one of the motorboats, the directional panel "Dover" in England, undoubtedly an allusion to invading the British Isles after the campaign in France, an operation that will be unceasingly postponed until finally being abandoned on October 12, 1940. *UBA*

U-30, which had asked for a supply of torpedoes by radio on July 4, 1940, is the first U-boat sent to Lorient. On July 7, it passes in front of the citadel of Port-Louis with six pennants fixed on the periscope floating in the wind; each flag represents a ship the commander considered sunk. From afar the smoke from fuel barrel fires at Priatec in Lanester. *AC*

## *July 1940: Arrival of the First Six U-boats*

JULY 1940

| U-BOATS | TYPE | FLOT. | COMMANDER | ARRIVAL | DEPART | NOTES |
|---|---|---|---|---|---|---|
| **U-30** | VIIA | 2 | Fritz-Julius Lemp | 7 24 | 13 | first arrival in Lorient, put into service 8.10.36; sank the liner *Athenia* on September 3, 1939, first victim in the battle of the Atlantic |
| **U-34** | VIIA | 2 | Wilhelm Rollmann | 18 | 23 | first arrival in Lorient, put into service 12.9.36; Final departure: turned into a school ship, sunk during a collision, refloated and relegated 8.9.43. Score: 21 cargo ships, 1 destroyer, 1 submarine and 1 minesweeper sunk |
| **U-99** | VIIB | 7 | Otto Kretschmer | 21 | 25 | first arrival in Lorient, put into service 18.4.40 |
| **U-52** | VIIB | 7 | Otto Salman | 21 | 27 | first arrival in Lorient, put into service 4.2.39 |
| **U-56** | IIC | 1 | Otto Harms | 21 | 25 | first arrival in Lorient, put into service 26.11.38 |
| **U-58** | IIC | 1 | Heinrich Schonder | 22 | 29 | first arrival in Lorient, put into service 4.2.39 |

***Movements***: seven arrivals, six departures, number of U-boats present at the end of the month of July 1940 in Lorient: one.

***Observations***: On July 2, the U-boat Corps Command General Staff returned from its inspection of French ports. *Konteradmiral* Dönitz immediately sent a report on the subject to German Navy High Command. He specified that his General Staff should be transferred France as soon as possible and that the phases for setting up a base in Lorient were the following: 1.) the possibility of being supplied with fuel, water and food; 2.) the possibility of carrying out small repairs; 3.) the transfer of the Command Post as soon as the first two measures had been carried out; 4.) the possibility of carrying out repairs on all the U-boats. On July 3, he stated that, cleared of the risk of magnetic mines by minesweepers from the 2nd *Räumboots-Flotilla*, the port in Lorient would be opened for U-boats on July 6. The next day, U-30 commanded by *Kapitänleutnant* Lemp, who had asked by radio for torpedoes, put into the port. The six U-boats that put into port in July only spent a few days in Lorient, the time to be supplied with torpedoes and fuel; there wasn't any question of carrying out any important work because the basins in the arsenal which had been sabotaged by the French Navy had just been taken in hand by the *Kriegsmarine*. The U-boats simply berthed at one of the ten places on the quay on the Scorff. One could berth alongside each of the floating platforms *"Audacieuse, Isère, Surveillante and Vaucluse"* while the *"Martinière and Psyche"* could take two U-boats each. The last platform, the old sloop *"Enseigne de vaisseau Henry,"* which dated back to World War I and which had been scuttled by the French on June 18, 1940, had been refloated by the Germans. Apart from U-99, which had been put into service in April 1940, the five other U-boats were old models put into service a long time before the war. In addition to two U-boats of the 2nd Flotilla, the four others belonged to the 1st and 7th Flotillas (two from each). Until May 1941, all U-boats that put into Lorient belonged to these three flotillas.

Until the end of 1940, the 1st U-Flotilla *Weddigen*, created in September 1935 with Kiel as its home port, regrouped the IIB, IIC and IID-type coastal U-boats. U-56 and U-58, IIC-type U-boats arriving in Lorient in July, hadn't been built for the huge waves in the Atlantic; with a length of 43.9 meters, which were nicknamed "Pirogues" by the submariners, lacked stability; the IIC-type, with its crew of twenty-five men, could sail 3,450 miles on the surface and carried a maximum of six torpedoes. Due to the lack of U-boats available at the epoch, they were sent to Lorient to hunt in the Atlantic. The crewmembers of four of them, U-56 to U-59, declared operational when the war began, hadn't yet finished their training period. Of the eight models of IIC-types built, six put into Lorient between July and October 1940 before being sent back to Germany and turned into school ships. Each of them had sunk a minimum of three ships and U-57 and U-59 had sunk more than fifteen. These good results were mainly due to the fact that the British still didn't have efficient defensive methods while the targets were still numerous. The 1st U-Flotilla which later used VIIC-type U-boats, was transferred to Brest in June 1941.

Before the war, the 2nd U-Flotilla *Saltzwedel*, created in September 1936 with Wilhelmshaven as its home port, regrouped the IA and VIIA-type U-boats and IX-types after January 1, 1940. After July 1940, this flotilla, commanded by *Korvettenkapitän* Heinz Fischer, was conjointly based between Wilhelmshaven and Lorient before being definitely transferred in June 1941. U-30 and U-34, arriving in Lorient in July, were VIIA-types of which only ten models had been built between 1935 and 1936. The VIIA-types measured 64.5 meters long and 5.8 meters wide. With a displacement of 626 tons on the surface and 745 tons while submerged, they had been built as attack U-boats in the high seas. They had a top speed of sixteen knots on the surface and eight knots maximum while submerged. Its normal crew consisted of forty-four men. Their armament comprised five torpedo-launching tubes, four in font and one behind; eleven torpedoes were carried on board. An 88mm gun was installed on the fore-deck and a 20mm *Flak* gun on the "tub" – the platform situated behind the conning tower. Its two weak points were its short action range of only 4,300 nautical miles and small number of torpedoes carried on board. Of the ten VIIA-types built, six put into Lorient between July and October 1940; As these U-boats had been engaged at a favorable time in spite of their design faults, each of them had ten ships sunk to their credit and two of them had sunk over twenty. Later they were turned into school ships for the Training Flotillas in the Baltic Sea.

Until mid-1940, 7th U-Flotilla *Wegener*, created in June 1938 with Kiel as home port, regrouped the VIIB-type U-boats. After the construction of the first ten VIIA-type U-boats, German engineers had studied this new, higher performance U-boat in 1937. Longer by two meters, the VIIB-type could stock thirty-three tons more fuel, which increased its action range. In all, twenty-four VIIB-type U-boats were built. In relation to the VIIA, the VIIB could travel 2,200 miles farther at a top speed of twelve on the surface, which increased its rayon of action to 6,500 miles. Its second interest was that it could carry fourteen torpedoes. In addition, it was easier to maneuver while submerged thanks to its two twin propellers and the increased power of its diesel engines made it 2½ times faster. U-48 and U-99 VIIB-types were the two U-boats that sank the most enemy tonnage during the two world wars with a total of over 550,000 tons. The 7th U-Flotilla, which was mainly supplied with the new VIIC-types at the end of 1940, was transferred to St. Nazaire during the first half of 1941.

***Allied Reactions***: The British didn't delay in reacting to the presence of U-boats in Lorient. During the first half of 1940, they were active on the maritime and aerial fronts, but with very limited means. On July 16 and 22, the Royal Air Force flew twice over the town during the day on reconnaissance to see the extent of the German Navy's use of the port and to decide what measures they should take. ■

*Korvettenkapitän* Heinz Fischer (second from the left), the Chief of the 2nd Flotilla, is climbs a ladder from the motorboat to U-30 to greet Commander Fritz-Lulius Lemp, who we can see in a white cap and scarf at the foot of the conning tower. Like thirteen other U-boat commanders to pass through Lorient, Lemp wasn't born in Germany; he was born in Tsingtao, China, the son of an officer stationed there. In the background is the citadel of Port-Louis. *UBA*

U-30, whose insignia is a frisky puppy, arrives at *La Glacière* Quay in the fishing port in Lorient; at the bottom on the left, is the tiny island of St. Michel. A fox terrier called *Schnurzl* belonging to Commander Lemp that accompanied him everywhere except on board which resulted in him asking Radioman Georg Högel to paint it on U-30's conning tower on September 10, 1939, so that it could virtually accompany him on patrols! The dog wasn't there on their return to Wilhelmshaven; it had been embarked as a mascot aboard a destroyer that hit a mine. As for Radioman Georg Högel, he followed Lemp on U-110 but survived the destruction of this U-boat by the British. He was taken prisoner on May 9, 1941; after the war, Georg Högel wrote a reference book on U-boat insignia (Schiffer Publishing, Ltd.). *Charita*

*Kapitänleutnant* Fritz-Julius Lemp enjoys a cigar after arriving in Lorient. The commander nicknamed "Lucky Lemp" by his crew, has just been interviewed by War Correspondent Kurt Esmarsch; in the background is Esmarsch's truck that serves as a recording studio. On September 3, 1939, Lemp accidently sank the passenger liner "*Athenia*" causing the death of 112 people, including twenty-eight Americans. Declaring on his return that he had really thought he was torpedoing an armed merchant ship (he wasn't authorized). The incident was kept secret in the U-boat Corps, and was openly and loudly condemned by the British. *LB*

During its stay in Lorient in July 1940, U-30, berthed with the motorboats-minesweepers in front of Péristyle barracks, is covered by large tarpaulins to camouflage it from air attacks. The six U-boats that passed through Lorient in July only stayed for about a week while being re-supplied; there was no question of doing important work in the port. *Charita*

**Left:** *Kapitänleutnant* Wilhelm Rollmann, commander of U-34 VIIA-type U-boat since 1938. This U-boat stopped in Lorient only once to be re-supplied between July 18 and July 23, 1940. Its logbook notes that it was berthed at the *Isère* on its arrival to get fuel and tinned food. On July 21, it loaded torpedoes and lubricating oil in the fishing port. It came back to the *Isère* on July 22 for ammunition and fresh food. On July 23, after Dönitz made an inspection tour aboard the U-boat at 08:30, U-34 left the port at 09:00 accompanied by motorboat-minesweepers. Just before its arrival at its homeport in Wilhelmshaven, it sunk the British submarine *HMS Spearfish* and took aboard its sole survivor. Under a previous commander, U-34 had already sunk the Spanish submarine C-3 off Malaga during the Spanish War in 1936! Commander Rollmann was awarded the Knight's Cross on July 31, 1940, for having sunk twenty-one cargo ships, one destroyer, one minesweeper, and one submarine. Sent as an instructor at the U-boat school, he was killed on November 5. In October 1940, U-34 was converted to a school U-boat until it sank in August 1943 after an accidental collision with a ship. It was refloated and put out of service the following month. *LB*

On July 23, 1940, U-99, a VIIB-type that had arrived two days earlier, had been summarily camouflaged on the Scorff. According to an account given by Chief Engineer Ehrhardt of U-52, this camouflage consisted of pieces of canvas cut from anti-aircraft balloons. U-99 was joined by U-58 IIC-type that had arrived the day before. The difference in size of the two U-boats is clearly visible. *UBA*

*Oberleutnant* Otto Harms commanded U-56 "pirogue" since January 1940. In August 1939, while their crews were still in training, the IIC U-56, 57, 58, and 59 IIC-type U-boats were declared operational to join the feeble combat force at Dönitz's disposal. After operating to the west of Scotland out of Lorient, U-56 was sent to the Baltic as a training U-boat in November 1940; at that time its score was four ships sunk and one damaged. After being an instructor, the commander was given the command of U-464 supply U-boat in April 1942; it was aboard this U-boat that he was taken prisoner during the same year. He died in 1980. *UBA*

Via Lorient on July 21, 1940, U-52 arrived in Kiel on August 13; during their stay in Lorient, the German marines picked up some French Navy bonnets that they wear with some panache on their arrival in Germany! *UBA*

German workers from the MAN Company repair the basins in the arsenal that the French soldiers had sabotaged in June 1940. Here basin No.2 will be the first in operation in mid-August. *UBA*

**Left:** On the left, Commander Otto Salman of U-52 wears a French War Cross above his pocket, while Chief Engineer Klaus Ehrhardt (center) wears his around his neck and has a French bonnet from "*Le Flibustier.*" This ship was docked in La Seyne-sur-Mer being fitted with weapons on June 23, 1940, but hadn't been finished; it was used in Toulon Harbor as a smoke generating platform until 1944. We can put forward the theory that after Toulon, it would have been bound for Lorient where the uniform service in depot No.5 had already prepared the bonnets with *"Le Flibustier"* printed on the ribbon. After being part of the crew aboard U-76 and U-161, Ehrhardt was named Chief Engineer of the 7th Flotilla in St. Nazaire. He died in 1990. *UBA*

## *August 1940: Five "Pirogues" in Lorient*

AUGUST 1940

| U-BOATS | TYPE | FLOT. | COMMANDER | ARRIVAL | DEPART | NOTES |
|---|---|---|---|---|---|---|
| **U-30** | VIIA | 2 | Fritz-Julius Lemp | 5 | | Final departure: turned into a school ship, scuttled 5.5.45. Score: 15 ships sunk and 2 damaged |
| | | | | ARRIVAL | | |
| **U-99** | VIIB | 7 | Otto Kretschmer \ Knight's Cross awarded on arrival | 5 | | U-99 remained 1 month in Lorient pour maintenance after its 3rd combat patrol |
| **U-57** | IIC | 1 | Erich Topp | 7 | 14 | First arrival in Lorient, put into service 29.12.38; Final departure: turned into school ship, scuttled the 3.5.45. Score: 15 ships sunk and 1 damaged |
| **U-37** | IXA | 2 | Viktor Oehrn | 12<br>30 | 17 | first arrival in Lorient, put into service 4.8.38; 1st U-boat to be put into a dry dock in Lorient |
| **U-58** | IIC | 1 | Heinrich Schonder | 12 | | |
| **U-56** | IIC | 1 | Otto Harms | 14 | 19 | Final departure: turned into a school ship, destroyed during Allied bombardment the 28.4.45. Score: 4 ships sunk, 1 damaged |
| **U-60** | IIC | 1 | Adalbert Schnee | 18 | 21 | First arrival in Lorient, put into service 22.7.39 |
| **U-65** | IXB | 2 | Hans-Gerrit von Stockhausen | 19 | 21 | first arrival in Lorient, put into service 15.2.40<br>Returns from special patrol with a spy |
| **U-59** | IIC | 1 | Joachim Matz | 19 | 26 | First arrival in Lorient, put into service 4.3.39; first U-boat taken out of the water on the slip-way in the fishing port |
| **U-48** | VIIB | 7 | Hans-Rudolf Rösing Knight's Cross awarded the next day | 28 | | First arrival in Lorient, put into service 22.4.39; change of commander, Rösing named Italian Liaison Officer |

On August 5, 1940, U-99 returns from its third combat patrol with seven pennants – each representing a ship sunk – and instead of the tonnage, it's the U-boat's insignia on the pennant. U-99 stayed for six months in the naval shipyards, whose repair service had come into operation three days earlier, for a complete overhaul. *LB*

On August 8, *Großadmiral* Erich Raeder, Commander-in-Chief of the German Navy, congratulates U-99's crew during the ceremony awarding the Knight's Cross to Commander Otto Kretschmer. The submariners are equipped with new British uniforms, because the uniforms they received during their last call in Lorient fell to pieces during their first evening in the port! They had been sabotaged with acid by the British before their departure that was activated by human body heat in the U-boat. In the background: the *Condé*, used as a depot in the Scorff. *UBA*

*Großadmiral* Raeder awards the Knight's Cross to Otto Kretschmer, who sunk at least 100,000 tons of shipping with the three U-boats he commanded since the beginning of the war. *LB*

Watched by *Vizeadmiral* Lothar von Arnauld de La Perrière, U-boat record-holder in World War I, awarded the "Merit" Cross and Commander of the German navy in Brittany, *Großadmiral* Raeder, accompanied by Kretschmer, congratulates U-99's crew. Lothar von Arnauld de La Perrière was killed in a plane crash in February of 1941. *UBA*

***Movements:*** Ten arrivals, seven departures, number of U-boats present in Lorient at the end of the month: four.

***Observations***: On August 2, 1940, the U-boat repairs service came into operation in Lorient; the deposit and supplies service that already existed was integrated into a new Unit – the *Kriegsmarinewerft Lorient* – an arsenal of the Navy commanded by *Vizeadmiral* Hans Stobwasser. On August 7, the war diary of the Command of U-boat Operations noted that a dry dock, sabotaged by the French and repaired by workers from the *MAN Company*, would be ready on the 12th to receive U-37, damaged by the British during its patrol. U-37 needed a complete overhaul that would take a month and U-58, which was leaving oil in its wake, needed to stay for three weeks. Apart from that, the six other U-boats only remained for a week in the port which they had put into for supplies. On August 8, 1940, *Großadmiral* Erich Raeder, Commander-in-Chief of the Kriegsmarine, visited Lorient; he wanted to see the port's capacities and to review the crew of U-57, which had arrived the day before. In addition, he was going to give, for the first time, the Knight's Cross to commander on the quay in front of Saltzwedel *Kaserne*. This decoration had been awarded on August 4 to *Kapitänleutnant* Otto Kretschmer, commander of U-99, following his report of tonnage sunk during his third combat patrol aboard this U-boat who had passed the 100,000 ton mark of ships destroyed necessary to obtain this distinction. He was the first commander to receive this decoration directly in Lorient. During their last call in this port at the end of July, the men of U-99 had been given British uniforms that had been abandoned in a depot when the British Expeditionary Force had left the port. While inspecting the crew, *Großadmiral* Raeder noted their ironic pride at being the most elegant crew, obviously because of their charming uniforms! Otto Kretschmer was nicknamed "*Silent Otto*" because of his reserve and because he was extremely cautious on the security level and only sent a few radio messages for fear of them being picked up by the British radio-locating service.

During the second half of August, U-59 IIC-type was the first to be taken out of the water using the slip-way infrastructure in the Kéroman fishing port. Of nine different U-boats that put into the port during the month, five were coastal

A crewmember of U-99 hangs the Knight's Cross around Kretschmer's neck. *Charita*

War correspondent Kurt Esmarsch asks a crewmember for details about U-99's last patrol; the discreet Commander Kretschmer had left to celebrate his decoration with his men with a beer on the U-boat's bridge. *UBA*

Between August 7 and 14, U-57 under Erich Topp and U-99 commanded by Kretschmer, alongside each other on the right bank of the Scorff, were camouflaged under large tarpaulin covers. On the left bank in the background, hold No.7 covered up, just behind hold No.5 inaugurated in 1913. U-57 stopped in Lorient only once. After thirteen patrols without incident, it was accidently rammed by a Norwegian ship just off Kiel, its homeport. The U-boat sank with six men on board, but was later refloated and used in U-boat training. Erich Topp later took command of U-522 aboard which he was awarded the Knight's Cross with Oak Leaves and Swords in August 1942. After this, he took a post on land before becoming commander of a XXI-type U-boat at the end of the war. He died in 2005. *UBA*

On August 12, 1940, U-37 arrives for the first time in Lorient; it has just berthed on the Scorff, along the old U-boat wharf, next to hold No.7 on the left bank where the welcome committee is waiting. In 1939, this U-boat, the first IXA-type out of the shipyards, had participated, along with U-46 and U-48, in the first communal attack of three U-boats against a convoy. Five U-boats were supposed to have taken part in this attack, but two of them were sunk before reaching their goal. *UBA*

IIC-types nicknamed "*pirogues*." For the second month running, of the six U-boats arriving in Lorient for the first time, five were put into service before the war save for a single one built in 1940. In spite of the arrival of several U-boats there were only four at the end of the month. This was due to three early VIIA and IIC-types put into service between 1936 and 1938 being recalled from the Front and turned into school ships. On August 20, Admiral Dönitz moved U-boats monitoring line slightly to the west away from the coast to avoid British aviation based on land. On August 26, spent the night in Lorient in the *Terminus* Hotel; during the evening he met with the different U-boats' commanders present in the port to announce astonishing news: he had received the orders for the invasion of Britain planned for September 15! If the operation was put into effect, the U-boats in the Atlantic should return to Cherbourg to receive supplies of torpedoes; they would be used to prevent any British warships coming from the west to penetrate the Channel, leaving the passage free for the troopships to be used in the landing. An envelope containing all the orders, only to be opened in the event of receiving the radio message "See-Löwe" (Sea lion) signaling the start of the landing, was given to the commanders. The date of this operation was to be endlessly put back because the German Air Force was never able to control British air space as they had sworn they would. The envelopes were destroyed following the abandonment of the invasion project on October 12, 1940.

With the arrival of U-37 and U-65, the first IX-types put into Lorient. U-37, the first IXA-type U-boat out of the shipyards, had been put into service on August 4, 1938. Its main differences to the VII-type were to be found in its greater length and its more powerful motors. Longer than the VII-type by ten meters, it could carry more fuel thereby increasing its action range to 8,100 miles on the surface, which was almost double that of the VIIA; it could also carry twice as many torpedoes: twenty-two units. Thanks to its powerful diesel engines, it had a top speed of 18.3 knots on the surface. Its only disadvantage was its size: it took longer to dive and as a little difficult to maneuver. Of eight IXA-types built, three put into Lorient after August 1940; U-37 and U-38 left Lorient before the end of 1941 to be turned into school ships. U-43 was the only one to carry out operational patrols in 1942. All three obtained excellent results with a combined total of over 100 ships sunk.

The U-65, put into service in February 1940, was an IXB-type. A little larger than the IXA, it could carry eleven tons of extra fuel, which increased its action range by 600 miles. Fourteen IXB-types were built and all were assigned to the 2nd Flotilla where they were the most successful until the end of 1941. Of the fourteen IXB-types, only eleven put into Lorient, the other three, sunk during their first second patrols, didn't have the occasion. Four IXB-type U-boats of the 2nd Flotilla, U-103, U-107, U-123 and U-124, held the third to sixth places on the list of enemy tonnage sunk by U-boats. U-65 arrived in Lorient on August 19 with a curious extra passenger. He was the Irish agent, and member of the *IRA*, Frank Ryan,

In August 1940, U-99, whose horseshoe insignia can be seen, has been camouflaged by netting during its stay on the Scorff. *LB*

U-37, whose periscopes have been raised for maintenance, is berthed along the fuel tankers' wharf on the left bank opposite the oil dumps. In the background is Guesdon Bridge and a little farther, the railroad bridge. *Wolfgang Ockert*

who was to have been secretly disembarked on the Irish coast to work for *Abwehr*. This German espionage service had released him from a Spanish prison where he had been condemned to for life for fighting with the Republicans! The patrol had been aborted because there were to be two agents but one died during the crossing, the day before the planned landing! The other was Sean Russell, an Irishman who had been in the U.S. before the war to collect money for the IRA. While in U-65, he complained of terrible stomach cramps on August 12; there was nothing in the first aid-kit to help him, and he died two days later. In addition, the U-boat was leaking oil so it had no choice but to head for a French port as soon as possible. After arriving in Lorient, the agent Ryan was repatriated to Berlin where he died four years later. This was the third U-boat of the 2nd Flotilla that was supposed to carry out a special patrol in Ireland; the two other patrols carried out by U-37 and U-38 a few months earlier had gone without mishap. U-37 succeeded in disembarking a German in Ireland in the night February 9/10, 1940 to forge links with the *IRA*. Agent Ernst Weber-Drohl had found his contact but had been arrested three months later in April. The second patrol had been carried out by U-38 which disembarked two German meteorologists in Ireland in the night of June 12/13, 1940. The first, Walter Simon, aged about sixty, was arrested almost immediately in spite of his new Australian identity. However, the second, who had an Irish passport because he had married an Irishwoman long before the war, sent weather reports from Dublin for a long time.

*Korvettenkapitän* Hans-Rudolf Rösing, commander of U-48, arrived in Lorient on August 28 and received the Knight's Cross the next day. He gave up his position as commander on U-48 because on September 4 when he was named General Staff Liaison Officer of the "Italian Submarine Forces in the Atlantic" based in Bordeaux. Following a proposition made by the Italians on July 24, and accepted the next day par the *Kriegsmarine*, the German and Italian Admiralties had signed a cooperation agreement: commanded by Admiral Parona, about forty Italian submarines put into Bordeaux on September 4 to reinforce U-boat battle in the Atlantic. The problem was that the Italian submarines hadn't been built for the Atlantic but for the calm waters of the Mediterranean, and their crewmembers hadn't been trained in collective attacks. Their results were more than disappointing: during October while each U-boat sank 920 tons a day, Italian submarines only sank twenty tons. At the end of December 1940, after several failed attempts at collective attacking with the German U-boats, the German and Italian General Staffs decided to place the Italian submarines first in the Mid and then the South Atlantic so they could act on their own with their own methods, which gave better results in 1941.

***Allied reactions***: An aerial reconnaissance patrol in full daylight was carried out on August 8; it was followed by tracts being dropped over the town in the night of August 10/11. On the maritime level, on August 20, 1940, at 01:16, the British submarine *HMS Cachalot*, hiding in ambush southwest of Groix Island, sent six torpedoes towards U-51 which was approaching Lorient. Two torpedoes hit U-boat which sank immediately with its entire crew of forty-three men. This U-boat of the 7th Flotilla, which had just finished its fourth combat patrol, had been commanded by *Kapitänleutnant* Dietrich Knorr. It had six ships sunk to its credit. In the war diary of the U-boat Corps Command, following U-51's missed rendezvous with its escort outside the port, it was noted that the U-boat had possibly been sunk by a mine. The 2nd Flotilla's minesweepers had checked the sector but hadn't found anything; in consequence, orders were given that the U-boats should only enter the port with an escort ship during the two hours preceding high tide and the two hours following it. To accompany U-boats when the weather was too bad for the powerful motorboats to set out, the ship *Rostock*, which was being turned into a blockade runner, was later assigned to Lorient.

The Battle of Britain, which began on August 12, 1940, occupied the British chaser for three months, until the Germans abandoned the idea of invading England. The bombers of the Bomber Command, which hadn't been directly concerned, began their raids on the French ports. When *Generalfeldmarschall* von Brauchitsch, Supreme Commander of the Army, spent the day in Lorient and the night in Kernével, the first British raid on Lorient took place in the night of August 22/23, 1940: twelve Hampden I planes of the 49th and 83rd Bombardment Groups dropped magnetic mines and a few bombs. The German anti-aircraft defenses placed on the highest points of the town were very active; these were 371th *Flak* Detachment who had arrived on August 16. However, *Konteradmiral* Dönitz thought that their reinforcement was necessary to efficiently protect the basins and his future command post. On July 24, the *Fliegerkorps IV* agreed to send a second detachment as soon as the situation of the Battle of Britain improved. The immediate decision taken after the British bombardment in the night was to close the port the next day, August 23, while the

Heinrich Schonder, commander of U-58, having a cup of coffee with his guests on the bridge. *UBA*

Between August 19 and 26, 1940, U-59 is the first German U-boat to be put into dry dock using the slipway system in the French fishing port. *UBA*

U-30 only called in Lorient twice: in July and August 1940. When it returned to its home base in Wilhelmshaven on August 27 to be turned into a U-boat trainer, its commander, Fritz-Julius Lemp, was awarded the Knight's Cross. His score was fifteen ships sunk and two damaged when he returned to Lorient in March 1941 as the commander of U-110. *Charita*

*Schnellboote* S-18-type motorboats are placed in the fishing port's channel that leads to the slipway we can see on the left in the background. Behind it in the forest is Kéroman Chateau. *LB*

By handing out three bottles of Cognac, Karl Heyne, Chief Engineer aboard U-59, has managed to convince three French workers to explain how the slipway in the fishing port works. With a German father and French mother, he spoke fluent French, which was a great help! He was lost at sea on December 16, 1941, as Chief Engineer aboard U-557. Seventy years later, in May 2011, accompanied by Benoît Senne, his two daughters Brigitte and Jutta retrace his steps back to Lorient. *Famille Heyne*

**Left:** Completely out of the water, U-59's hull is very vulnerable in the event of an air attack. The system of camouflage using tarpaulin stretched from the antennas is very primitive. *UBA*

August 22: *Generalfeldmarschall* von Brauchitsch, Commander-in-Chief of the German Army, visits Lorient Port. Accompanied by *Vizeadmiral* Hans Stobwasser, first director of the naval shipyard, he visits the installations on the Scorff aboard a motorboat. *LB*

August 28: U-48 approaching Lorient had to wait outside the port all day while the mines placed by the British the day before were eliminated. The men take advantage of this unexpected free time to sunbathe on the bridge. *Matroseobergefreiter* Kloruss, on the left, is wearing a British helmet. *UBA*

*Korvettenkapitän* Hans Rösing was commander of U-48 when it arrived in Lorient on August 28. Decorated with the Knight's Cross the following day, he was transferred to a ground post as liaison officer for the Italian Submarine General Staff in Bordeaux. Enlisting in the Navy in 1920, Rösing was one of the first commanders to have secretly served aboard the U-boats built abroad by German engineers between 1930 and 1931. *Charita*

U-51, commanded by Dietrich Knorr, didn't arrive in Lorient as expected. After its departure from Kiel on August 9, 1940, it was torpedoed on the surface by the British submarine *HMS Cachalot* southwest of Lorient and sunk. There were no survivors. *UBA*

Since July 1940, the motorboat minesweepers of the *2. Räumboots-flottille berthed* on the sloop *La Surveillante*, clear magnetic mines out of the access to Lorient Port. *LB*

These marines from U-48 stop at "*Chez Mélanie*" restaurant in Riec-sur-Belon. *Sascha Ulderup*

August 28, 1940: Passing Groix Island in its approach to Lorient, U-48 is escorted by a motorboat minesweeper from the *2. Räumboots-flottille. UBA*

Photo souvenir of U-48's crew after their meal at *"Chez Mélanie"* Restaurant. The submariners have a lot of money to spend when they return from patrols; their pay on arrival is increased by bonuses, notably when U-boats have spent days underwater. *Sascha Ulderup*

August 30, 1940: U-37 arriving in Lorient is escorted by a motorboat, which has past campaigns inscribed on it. *UBA*

A IIC-type U-boat kept on the Scorff was camouflaged by canvas stretched over each side of the antenna wire. *LB*

This VII-type U-boat, berthed at the *Isère* platform on the Scorff, waits for the replacement of the distilled water in its batteries that is stored in glass bottles in wicker baskets. *LB*

With seven victory pennants, U-37 passes the citadel of Port-Louis on August 30, 1940 after its seventh patrol. *UBA*

Members of U-37's crew, who stayed aboard on guard duty while their U-boat was in the fishing port, wash as best they can on the bridge. *UBA*

motorboats destroyed the mines that had been dropped. On the same day at 11:00, the minesweeper *La Montjoie* ran into a mine and three crewmembers were killed. It should be noted that a French minesweeping unit along with the German motorboats, helped clear the waters around Lorient. This was the 145th Minesweeping Section, a unit belonging to the French Minesweeper Center based in La Pallice, which had four sections under the authority of the Kriegsmarine in the search for magnetic mines. The section in Lorient, commanded by par Ensign 1st Class Gelard, worked until December 18, 1940, after which it was sent to La Rochelle; the four minesweeping sections were eventually sent to North Africa in June the following year. Finally, on August 27 between 02:05 and 03:00, eight Hampden I planes of the 49th and 83rd Bombardment Groups carried out a simultaneous bombardment and mine-laying patrol, notably targeting the railroads east of town. ■

## *September 1940: Prien, the "Bull of Scapa Flow"*

SEPTEMBER 1940

| U-BOOTE | TYPE | FLOT. | COMMANDER | ARRIVAL | DEPART | NOTES |
|---|---|---|---|---|---|---|
| **Present** | | | | | | |
| **U-37** | IXA | 2 | Viktor Oehrn | | 24 | |
| **U-48** | VIIB | 7 | Heinrich Bleichrodt | 25 | 8 | New commander |
| **U-58** | IIC | 1 | Heinrich Schonder | 20 | 2 | |
| **U-99** | VIIB | 7 | Otto Kretschmer | 25 | 4 | |
| Arrival | | | | | | |
| **U-100** | VIIB | 7 | Joachim Schepke Knight's Cross awarded on arrival | 1 \ 25 | 11 | First arrival in Lorient, put into service 16.3.40 |
| **U-59** | IIC | 1 | Joachim Matz | 3 \ 21 | 7 | |
| **U-38** | IXA | 2 | Hcinrich Liebe \ Knight's Cross awarded on arrival | 3 | 25 | First arrival in Lorient, put into service 24.10.38; |
| **U-46** | VIIB | 7 | Engelbert Endrass Knight's Cross awarded the day before and given on arrival | 6 | 20 | First arrival in Lorient, put into service 2.11.38; final departure, first U-boat to arrive in St. Nazaire the next day turned into school ship in August 1941 and scuttled 4.5.45. Score: 27 ships sunk, 5 damaged |
| **U-60** | IIC | 1 | Adalbert Schnee | 6 | 16 | Final departure turned into a school ship, scuttled 2.5.45. Score: 3 ships sunk and 1 damaged |
| **U-32** | VIIA | 2 | Hans Jenisch | 8 | 18 | First arrival in Lorient, put into service 5.4.37 |
| **U-61** | IIC | 1 | Wolf-Harro Stiebler | 15 | 24 | First arrival in Lorient, put into service 12.8.39; final departure, turned into a school ship and scuttled the 2.5.45. Score: 6 ships sunk and 1 damaged |
| **U-124** | IXB | 2 | Georg-Wilhelm Schulz | 16 | | First arrival in Lorient, put into service 11.6.40 |
| **U-101** | VIIB | 7 | Fritz Frauenheim Knight's Cross awarded on arrival | 16 | | First arrival in Lorient, put into service 11.3.40; |
| **U-28** | VIIA | 2 | Günter Kuhnke Knight's Cross awarded the 19.09 | 17 | | First arrival in Lorient, put into service 12.9.36; |
| **U-65** | IXB | 2 | Hans-Gerrit von Stockhausen | 25 | | |
| **U-47** | VIIB | 7 | Günther Prien | 26 | | First arrival in Lorient, put into service 17.12.38 |
| **U-138** | IID | 1 | Wolfgang Lüth | 26 | | First arrival in Lorient, put into service 27.6.40 |
| **U-137** | IID | 1 | Herbert Wohlfahrt | 29 | | First arrival in Lorient, put into service 15.6.40 |

On September 3, Commander Heinrich Liebe is the second commander to receive the Knight's Cross on his arrival in Lorient. He was awarded the decoration on August 14, according to the German communiqué of that period, for having, "*sunk sixteen ships totaling 97,296 tons, most of them were part of an escorted convoy.*" *LB*

Heinz Fischer, Chief of the 2nd Flotilla, aboard U-100's bridge, welcomes Commander Schepke and his Watch Officer, *Oberleutnant-zur-See* Günther Krech. *UBA*

In Lorient on September 2, Dönitz awards decorations to members of the U-59 crew on the Place d'Armes in front of the Gabriel pavilion. This IIC U-boat has already been on eleven patrols since August 1939, and will make two more before being transformed into a training boat. *LB*

The insignia of U-38 is Cupid, which refers to the commander's name: "Liebe" means "love" in German.

***Movements***: nineteen arrivals, eleven departures, number of U-boats present at the end of the month in Lorient: twelve.

***Observations***: An important number of arrivals during the month, berthing time in Lorient increased to 10-15 because the arsenal was congested. Like the previous month, three old types were turned into school ships. Of eleven new U-boats arriving for the first time in Lorient, six were early types built before the war and five had been built in 1940. At that time, U-boats were getting good results in the Western Approaches sector, and five commanders were awarded the Knight's Cross for theoretically passing 100,000 tons of enemy ships sunk. The decoration, often awarded following a particularly positive report sent from the commander by radio during his patrol, was given as soon as he reached the port in front of a crowd of soldiers and workers who had been informed of the arrival of a new "Ace." An Honor Guard – the Defense of Fortifications Company of the *Kriegsmarinewerft* – and a brass band welcomed the returning hero; during the first months the brass band came from the Army's 211th Infantry Division based in the Lorient sector since July 1940; later it was replace by a naval brass band assigned to the 2nd U-boat Flotilla.

In his war diary on September 3, *Vizeadmiral* Dönitz, who had left his command post in Sengwarden near Wilhelmshaven two days earlier and had moved into 18 Boulevard Suchet, Paris, noted: "*I got the following impressions during my short stay in Lorient: 1.) The lodgings for the* 2nd Flotilla *need to be improved and work is in hand. The lodgings for the crewmembers in Lorient itself are very good and they have R &R hotels*

U-37, which had been damaged by bombs during its seventh patrol, stayed for three weeks in Lorient in September for repairs. Its crew took advantage of this unexpected break to spend some of their leave in the Quiberon sea resort. *UBA*

Members of U-37's crew on Quiberon beach in September 1940. U-37's logbook noted that the first half of the crew was on leave from September 4 to 8, and the second half from September 8 to 12. *UBA*

Between September 2 and September 7, U-37 was put into dry dock in basin No.2 in the arsenal to have its hull repaired. *Wolfgang Ockert*

*in Quiberon. 2.) The danger represented by mines and enemy submarines is great and will necessitate constant important forces. 3.) The anti-aircraft defenses have proved to be inadequate following the last attack. Five British planes were able to fly at about 300 meters over the shipyards and drop ten bombs which fell very close to the U-boats; there is a gap in the north and northeast of Lorient through which the British have the habit of passing; a third anti-aircraft battery should be affected there. In any case, there is a lack of small caliber guns in the arsenal itself to fight against planes flying at low altitude, and this should be corrected immediately. All in all the port in Lorient is an entirely usable and valuable base, but it will be difficult to hold more than 10-15 U-boats at a time in repairs; in addition this number would provoke congestion and would put them at risk until the danger from planes is resolved. It is necessary to take over other bases on the Atlantic coast* for the new U-boat flotillas." On 5 September, the commander of the German Navy Erich Raeder was received at the U-boat HQ in Paris. After discussing the situation, Dönitz brought to his attention the urgency of sending more anti-aircraft defenses to Lorient; the Commander-in-Chief of the Navy thought about it and then said that he would give the necessary orders. Indeed, Admiral Dönitz noted on September 18: "*During a visit to Lorient, I saw that following the action taken by the Commander-in-Chief of the Navy, the anti-aircraft defenses have been reinforced; this has been felt during the last night attacks carried out by the British, their planes were prevented from flying over the base at low altitude.*"

On September 25, U-99, U-48, U-65, and U-100 arrived almost at the same time in Lorient between 10:09 and 10:45. *Kapitänleutnant* Joachim Schepke, commander of U-100 was given the Knight's Cross, which had been awarded by radio message the day before, directly on his arrival. He had already carried out three patrols as commander of U-3 and five patrols on U-19, IIA and IIB-type U-boats, with which he had sunk eleven ships. He had then been given the command of U-100 VIIB-type in May 1940 and had just finished his second patrol aboard this U-boat. During his two patrols, he had sunk thirteen ships and damaged another, which pushed him over the 100,000 tons mark. Thus he entered the closed circle of commanders holding the Knight's Cross. His rather easy-going style, notably concerning disciplinary rules, was appreciated by Dönitz who was always trying to build up a feeling of team spirit among his submariners. His good looks earned him the nickname: "Her Majesty's best-looking officer." He eased relations between his officers, petty officers, and his men by sending them all on leave together as soon as they arrived; he had even obtained the creation of a cleaning crew in the arsenal to take care of the U-boat when it arrived so that his men could take full advantage of their time ashore. Before any departure, he would organize a big party with his crew, where alcohol flowed to the beat of American jazz; Schepke had a collection of this type of music in his U-boat!

In Germany, jazz was officially considered "decadent," but ironically a jazz orchestra had

Once the work was finished on September 7, the dock was flooded so that U-37 could leave. On September 12, U-37's logbook noted that the U-boat would remain in the shipyards for another eight days while waiting for spare parts and a battery to be delivered; the crew was immediately granted a short leave in Germany. *Wolfgang Ockert*

The hotel "*Penthièvre et Plage*" in Quiberon was requisitioned to house crews on leave while their U-boats were under repair. *UBA*

At the beginning of the occupation, the *Beauséjour* Hotel, on the *Place Alsace-Lorraine* in Lorient, was used by the U-boat officers, while the crew mostly used the *Pigeon Blanc* Hotel. *UBA*

On September 6, 1940, the Knight's Cross was awarded to Commander Engelbert Endrass of U-46, directly upon his arrival in Lorient. He was the former Watch Officer aboard U-47 during the *Scapa Flow* raid. On the left, Commander Heinrich Bleichrodt of U-48 helps him put on the decoration. U-46 left Lorient on September 20, 1940, to join its new home base in St. Nazaire; it was the first U-boat to arrive at this port. After fifteen patrols it was turned into a U-boat trainer. Endrass, later decorated with the Knight's Cross with Oak Leaves, took over the command of U-567 on board which he was killed when it was sunk on December 21, 1941. *Charita*

U-37's motto, *"Westward-ho!,"* is shown on its conning tower as it makes final preparations on the right bank of the Scorff before departure. This Viking cry was painted on the conning tower on the orders of Commander Werner Hartmann. On the other side we can see the covered holds No.7 and No.5. *Coll; Anthony Guychard*

Early September: *FunkMaat* Wilhelm Kruse of U-48 has a drink on the terrace of the *St. Cornély* Hotel in Quiberon. Radioman Kruse later served aboard U-181 and was decorated with the German Cross in Gold on July 28, 1942. He died in 1991. *UBA*

*Obersteuermann* Herbert Engel, chief boatswain aboard U-48, on the terrace of the *St. Cornély* Hotel. He became Watch Officer aboard U-559 between February 1941 and March 1942, and then Commander of U-666 (nicknamed *U-Satan* because of the number – his family name, "Engel," is the German word for "angel") from August 1942 to December 1943. From September to October 1944 he commanded U-228. Decorated with the German Cross in Gold on November 9, 1943, he survived the war and died in 1991. *UBA*

On September 8, 1940, Walter Heyer, *MaschObergefreiter* aboard U-32, mounts the guard of his U-boat that has arrived for the first time in Lorient. This submariner has just been decorated with the Iron Cross 2nd Class following his seventh combat patrol aboard U-32, which had sunk three cargo ships and damaged a cruiser. *UBA*

U-boat Operations Command moved into 18 Boulevard Suchet in Paris on September 1st. *Konteradmiral* Dönitz had a bust of himself made by the sculptor Wolfgang Nieder. This sculpture was then sent to Kernével to do busts of the "Aces" for a memorial project for German submariners; this project never saw the light of day. *Bernd Siepert*

After guard duty, it's time for rest in Carnac. In front of the *Garage de la Plage*, accompanied by *MaschOMt* Philippezyk, Walter Heyer borrows a horse from an army unit. He has sewn the ribbon of his Iron Cross on the buttonhole of his jacket. *UBA*

been set up at the beginning of the War on Goebbels' orders. Called "*Charlie and his Orchestra*," it comprised excellent German musicians who made the dance floors swing with famous American songs, but parodying the lyrics! One of the best known, to the tune of "*Stormy weather*," imitated Churchill complaining about losses caused by U-boats: "*Don't know why, it's no matter how I try ... stormy weather ... since those U-boats are aiming better, just can't keep my ships together, they're sinking all the time.*" These songs were aired on Radio Hamburg which specifically aimed at foreign countries on short wave band, the Germans couldn't tune in on it. Several Americans who had gone over to the Germans broadcast programs in English: the three best known were Douglas Chandler, William Joyce, nicknamed "Lord Haw Haw" and American actress Mildred Gillard known in Germany under the name of "Axis-Sally"! The programs produced by Radio Hamburg were listened to throughout the world at the epoch, even in England where "Lord Haw Haw" was very famous! The last known song by "*Charlie and his Orchestra*" came out in 1943: "*Let's go bombing*."

The U-47 put into Lorient on September 26, 1940; at the epoch it was already the best-known U-boat. Its perilous action in the British military port of Scapa Flow in October 1939, during which it sank the battleship *Royal Oak*, had made it famous throughout Germany. Its commander, Günther Prien, was the first officer in the *Kriegsmarine* to be awarded the Knight's Cross on October 18, 1939. All the German personnel in Lorient, for whom Prien was a national hero, hurried to watch his arrival and have their photo taken at his side. They also wanted to see the conning tower of his U-boat whose insignia was a smoking bull: the "Bull of Scapa Flow." Prien was shown in newsreels in cinemas all over Germany and had been granted special permission to write a widely distributed book about his special patrol in *Scapa Flow*! During his previous patrol in mid-June 1940, he had been sent with five other U-boats to intercept the HX-48 convoys signaled

Loading torpedoes aboard U-100. Its 88mm gun had to be turned around to get the torpedoes inside. On the left: reserves of distilled water for the batteries. *UBA*

*Obergefreiter* Wilhelm Schmidt and *MaschObGef* Horst Schaper of U-100 on guard duty, wearing captured British uniforms in Lorient. During the destruction of their U-boat on March 17, 1941, Schaper survived and was taken prisoner, but Schmidt was KIA. *UBA*

On September 16, 1940, U-61, which had arrived the day before, is berthed alongside U-38 and camouflaged with tarpaulin stretched across its antenna wire. *UBA*

Departure of U-100 on September 11, 1940. On the left: Watch Officer Günther Krech, and on the right, Commander Schepke. As the latter had a habit of upping the tonnage of the ships he sank, the commanders got into the habit of saying when a U-boat came back with exaggerated successes, *"It's a tonnage worthy of Schepke!"* *UBA*

After their arrival of September 16, 1940, these crewmembers from U-101 celebrate their successes with champagne on the terrace of the *St. Cornély* Hotel in Quiberon. On the left is Commander Fritz Frauenheim. *LB*

On the Scorff, U-32 is made ready for its departure on operations. *UBA*

During September and October of 1940, most commanders arriving at Lorient took the train to Paris to make their reports. Dönitz is shown walking with his staff in the park near his headquarters. The commanders also benefitted from their Parisian stopover by visiting the many cabarets of the capital! *Bernd Siepert*

by the German surveillance service *B-Dienst*, but the convoy had been rerouted south of their position; this had been the first wolfpack to be formed after the first try-out in November 1939. When U-47 arrived in Lorient that September 26, it had just finished its seventh patrol during which the first real wolfpack attack had taken place since the beginning of the war. It had been carried out following *B-Dienst* deciphering a British radio message which gave the general location where a convoy was to meet its escort. Carried out against the SC-2 convoy on September 6, the operation had nevertheless been hampered by stormy weather with force eight winds and the appearance of British planes. U-47 succeeded in sinking four ships in the convoy, U-28 only one, while U-65 had been kept at distance by a British plane. On September 27, U-47 spotted the HX-72 convoy towards which he guided U-43, U-48, U-65, U-99 and U-100; until September 22, eleven ships in this convoy were sunk and one was damaged; U-100 alone sank seven ships in three hours! The crewmembers aboard the U-boats efficiently put into practice all wolfpack attack training in the Baltic Sea in peace-time. The HX-72 was the first convoy of the war to lose six ships or more; from then until the end of 1941, only three other convoys sustained such heavy losses. U-47's crew went into town after their arrival in Lorient on September 26; the officers were lodged in *Beauséjour* Hotel on the *Place Alsace-Lorraine*. During the evening of their second day the first important British bombardment on the town took place. None of the crewmembers were hurt and the concrete personnel shelter in *Salztwedel Kaserne* was put into good use. The three "Aces" Prien, Kretschmer and Schepke, who all belonged to the 7th Flotilla, knew each other very well. Between September 26 and October 12, it was the first time they had been together on land since leaving Germany and they celebrated their reunion at the restaurant "*Chez Mélanie*" in Riec-sur-Belon.

Two letters indicating their port of departure and arrival, followed by the convoy's number, indicated convoys going to or coming from England: for example the code SC-2 indicated the second convoy out of Sydney via Canada to England. Other convoy codes often found were HX: Halifax – England; HG: Gibraltar – England; OG: England – Gibraltar; ON: Liverpool – North America. The code OB indicated convoys out of Liverpool; escorted to a zone in the west judged secure, from there they could head in any direction. With the advance of U-boats towards the west, these convoys stopped in July 1941.

With the arrival of U-137 and U-138 at the end of the month, the first IID-types appeared in Lorient. The main improvement on the IIC was the larger hull qui which allowed it to carry an extra fifteen tons of fuel. It also increased its action range on the surface from 1,900 to 3,450 miles. But the IID was still too short at forty-four meters, which made it a little unstable in the water; too slow with its top speed of 12.7 knots on the surface and it only carried six torpedoes. Of the sixteen IID-types built, three put into Lorient and had

On September 16, 1940, Commander Fritz Frauenheim of U-101 received the Knight's Cross on the *Place d'Armes* in Lorient. Dönitz shakes his hand; behind him is Hartmann who was 1st Officer of the U-boat Corps General Command's General Staff from May 7 to October 31, 1940. After commanding U-37 and then occupying various posts in the *Kriegsmarine*, Hartmann was named Chief of the *Volkssturm* at the end of the war for the defense of Danzig Port against the Red Army, a post for which he was awarded the Oak Leaves to his Knight's Cross. He died in 1963. *LB*

Fritz Frauenheim thanks his officers and the Navy officers in front of one of Gabriel Hotel's pavilions. As commander of U-21 at the beginning of the war, he managed to drop mines in front of a British port and one of them badly damaged the British cruiser *HMS Belfast*. *UBA*

A fresco was created as a souvenir of this meeting: the different protagonists have signed their name under their portrait. We can see the five officers present in the preceding photo, as well as on the bottom on the right, Commander Wolf-Harro Stiebler of U-61, who arrived in Lorient on September 15th. *UBA*

On September 19, 1940, in Boulevard Suchet, Paris Günter Kuhnke, commander of U-28, arrived in Lorient two days earlier, receives the Knight's Cross from Admiral Dönitz following five successful patrols. *Charita*

Second half of September: crewmembers of U-28 pass their leave in Quiberon. From left to right: unknown, Winkler, *FkMt* Willi Anderheiden, and Hölterscheidt sitting down. *UBA*

U-58, which arrived in Lorient on September 20, is hoisted onto the slipway in the fishing port. This U-boat, which had already spotted a British submarine off Lorient when it left on September 2, was missed by the torpedo from a Royal Navy submarine on its return! *UBA*

satisfying results with a total of sixteen ships sunk and four damaged. U-137, U-138 and U-141 left the French port in August 1941.

For a question of logistics, the U-boat bases in France were specialized in the maintenance and repairs of a single type of U-boat. Lorient, which accommodated the 2nd Flotilla, received IX-types in priority. But, while waiting for the bases in Brest and St. Nazaire to become operational and sufficient ocean-going U-boats replaced the "pirogues," the II and VII –types were also as numerous.

***Allied reactions***: From 22:30 to midnight on September 1, twelve Hampden I bombers dropped their bombs on the port in the presumed position where the German U-boats were to be found. In fact, the bombs fell on the fishing port near the slip-way and several French ships were damaged and a French marine was killed. The Blenheim IV bombers took the relay in the night of September 2/3; three planes dropped their bombs which fell near Pont Gueydon while others destroyed an anti-aircraft post on the roof of a house. On September 17, Hampden planes laid eight magnetic mines. In the night of September 27/28, with thirty-five Hampden Is and Whitleys, Bomber Command ordered an air raid that killed thirty-two civilians and over a dozen Germans; twenty-nine houses were also destroyed. In his war diary, the commander of the U-boat Corps noted that if the port installations had sustained little damage, several submariners and land personnel had been killed, notably the soldiers using an anti-aircraft gun mounted on a truck in the middle of the *Place Alsace-Lorraine*. Three other attacks were carried out until the end of the month: at dawn on the

*Kapitänleutnant* Wolf-Harro Stiebler, commander of U-61, buys embroideries in Quiberon. He took command of U-461, a XIV-type used for re-supplying other U-boats. He died in 1991. *UBA*

Commanders Schulz of U-124 and Stiebler of U-61 in front of a beach hut in Quiberon. *UBA*

Reinhard "Teddy" Suhren, Watch Officer aboard U-48. After his brother, he was the second officer aboard a U-boat to receive the Knight's Cross without being a commander. This decoration was awarded on November 3, 1940, for having sunk over 200,000 tons worth of ships under three different commanders. It was his third commander, Bleichrodt, with whom he had sunk eight ships, who insisted on this award. Commander Bleichrodt had been awarded the Knight's Cross on October 24, but he refused to wear it if his Watch Officer didn't receive the same decoration. Suhren returned to Lorient at the end of 1941 as commander of U-564. *Charita*

On September 25, 1940, four U-boats arrive in Lorient almost simultaneously between 10:09 and 10:45. U-48, U-99 and U-65 are the first to pass the citadel in Port-Louis; U-100 arrived fifteen minutes later. *UBA*

U-65 arrives in Lorient, returning from its fourth patrol with two victory pennants. This U-boat, which stopped over in Lorient the previous month, was the first IXB-type to call at the port. *UBA*

On September 25, 1940, U-99 arrives in Lorient, returning from its fourth combat patrol. On Dönitz's orders, Commander Kretschmer took Italian Commander Longobardo onboard to familiarize him with German attack methods. Discussions with Kretschmer aboard the U-boat were in English, which wasn't a problem for the commander who had studied the language in 1929 at the University of Exeter in the south of England. *Bernd Siepert*

On September 26, Prien's U-47 arrives in its turn. With Schepke's U-100 arrival day before, the 7th Flotilla's three most decorated commanders are reunited in Lorient for the first time since they'd left Germany. The bull insignia was painted by Watch Officer Endrass on their return from their raid on the British port of Scapa Flow in October 1939, where U-47 sunk the battleship *Royal Oak*. This action made the U-boat and its crew famous throughout Germany. Commander Prien was granted special permission to write his memories and have them published. *LB*

28th by three Blenheims, which bombed the port and laid mines; the same day at 21:10 by five Beauforts which dropped bombs in the same zone, and finally on the 30th when two planes dropped mines off Lorient.

On the maritime level, on September 2, while leaving Lorient U-58 spotted a British submarine in the BF 6177 square. To locate their ships in the ocean, the German Navy had divided sea charts into large squares indicated by two letters: for example, the prefix BF corresponded to the Bay of Biscay, AN to the North Sea. These large squares were then re-divided into 81 squares numbered from 11 to 19 and then 21 to 29, etc up to 91 to 99. The zone BF 61 corresponded to the coast off Lorient; it was re-divided according to the same principle into 81 squares, which meant that the zone BF 6177 precisely located the British submarine. Certainly no coincidence, on September 10 an article with three color photos under the title *"Submarine fishermen at work"* appeared in *Signal*, a German magazine printed in French and widely distributed. The article explained that barriers of steel netting attached to buoys were to prevent enemy submarines from penetrating the entrance to the ports. In reaction to the presence of enemy submarines off Lorient, two submarine chasers put into port on September 12. The U-boat Corps Command explained their task and gave them a first hunting zone around Pen March, and this sector was prohibited to German U-boats. But on September 20, U-58 returning to Lorient was surprised by a British "Clyde" submarine during the night at a distance of only 200 meters, which fired a torpedo at U-58. In fact, there were two British submarines in the sector! On September 24, *HMS Cachalot* laid fifty mines in the sector around Pen March while *HMS Tuna* torpedoed the German catapult ship *Ostmark* off Belle Ile; this ship, built in 1936, had left Verdon for Brest where it had been going to be used, with its plane for air reconnaissance. On September 26, U-138 was attacked while approaching Lorient by a British submarine which fired four torpedoes but without success; returning with U-47, the two U-boats were attacked by an enemy plane but without any particular damage. Dönitz noted in his war diary: *"Following these two attacks, I am forced to ask for escorts for my U-boats entering or leaving the port, so that enemy submarines will be forced to dive before their passage and so that our U-boats will be protected from enemy air attack. This request cannot be granted for the moment due to a lack of planes, but I shall repeat the demand for the constitution of bases on the Atlantic coast with devices reserved for the Navy."*

The first French intelligence systems started their activities in September 1940. Already at the end of July, the wife of French General Duhautois, named Police Director of the Lorient zone on June 12, was hailed in the street by a German captain; he turned out to be a former Legionnaire who had served under her husband in Cochin China! His name was Hermann, and he told her that he worked for the French Army's intelligence service. For over two years he passed numerous messages to his former chief, mainly about U-boat movements and the construction of the base. In Vichy in September, Commander Trautmann, Chief of the north section of the French Navy's *Deuxième Bureau* recruited Engineer 1st Class of the Maritime Engineers, Jacques Stosskopf. Born in Alsace and speaking fluent German, Stosskopf, who had access to the entire arsenal, faithfully informed him of everything happening there; his reports were then sent to the American Embassy in Vichy. Commander Jean Duplessis de Grénédan who even recruited two German informers, set up a third intelligence network at the same time. At the end of the year, the *"Confrérie Notre Dame"* set up by the famous Gilbert Renault *alias Colonel Rémy* and *"Nemrod"* Reseaux also had agents in Lorient. Finally, a Czech-born German woman, working as a secretary for the *Kommandantur* in the Chamber of Commerce building, got information from the prostitutes visited by the German submariners, which she then passed on to the British. ■

Though some of the general staff, like Oehrn, regarded Prien as being somewhat "hotheaded" – "Bumskopf" – Dönitz liked him a great deal. For the birth of his daughter, he sent the following message to him personally: "*Ein U-Boot ohne Sebrohr STI heute angekommen*" ("U-boat without a periscope arrived today"). Like several other commanders trained during peacetime, Prien came from the merchant marine. Behind him is war correspondent Wolfgang Frank. *LB*

Wolfgang Frank, on the left, questions Herbert Schultze and Günther Prien. Herbert Schultze, after his fifth patrol as commander of U 48, had fallen seriously sick and was in the hospital from May to the end of September 1940. He was the second U-boat commander to receive the Knight's Cross after Prien. *LB*

On 25 September 1940 at the Place d'Armes, after awarding the Chevalier Cross to Joachim Schepke, *Vizeadmiral* Dönitz awards Iron Crosses to members of the crew. *UBA*

In the night of September 27/28, the British carried out their first large scale air raid on Lorient with thirty-five planes; twenty-nine houses were destroyed. A bomb fell on the *rue des Fontaines*. *LB*

Second half of September: *Kapitänleutnant* Otto Kretschmer, wearing his white walking-out dress, chats with an officer of the 2nd Flotilla's ground staff in front of *l'Armor Bar* on the ground floor of the *Grand Hotel* in Carnac. Although discreet, Kretschmer was not without humour: during a patrol as commander of U-23 at the beginning of the war, he fired a torpedo at a rock that, from far off, resembled a cruiser. Rather than keep it secret, he sent the following message, "*Felsen torpediert aber nicht versenkt*" ("rock torpedoed but not sunk."). Thinking that the radio operator of U-99 had made a mistake on the first word, the message, "*Nelsen torpediert,*" was retransmitted to Dönitz, who thought that it meant the British battleship *Nelson.* On his return to Germany, Kretschmer and Dönitz laughed at the joke, but they had to contact the Propaganda Ministry to tell them not to communicate the sinking of the battleship *Nelson,* which they had been about to do! *UBA*

Army trousers and boots were lent to these three U-99 officers so they could go riding. *UBA*

Officers of U-99 horse riding on the beach at Carnac with general staff officers of the 317th Infantry Regiment, 211th Infantry Division. Bonds were forged between U-99 and this regiment, which would later "sponsor" the U-boat. *UBA*

On September 29th, U-137 arrived in Lorient. During its first combat patrol, this IID-type U-boat, commanded by Herbert Wolhfahrt nicknamed "*Parzival,*" sank three ships and damaged a fourth west of the British Isles. Its insignia represents the knight Parsifal sinking a ship with his thumb. *LB*

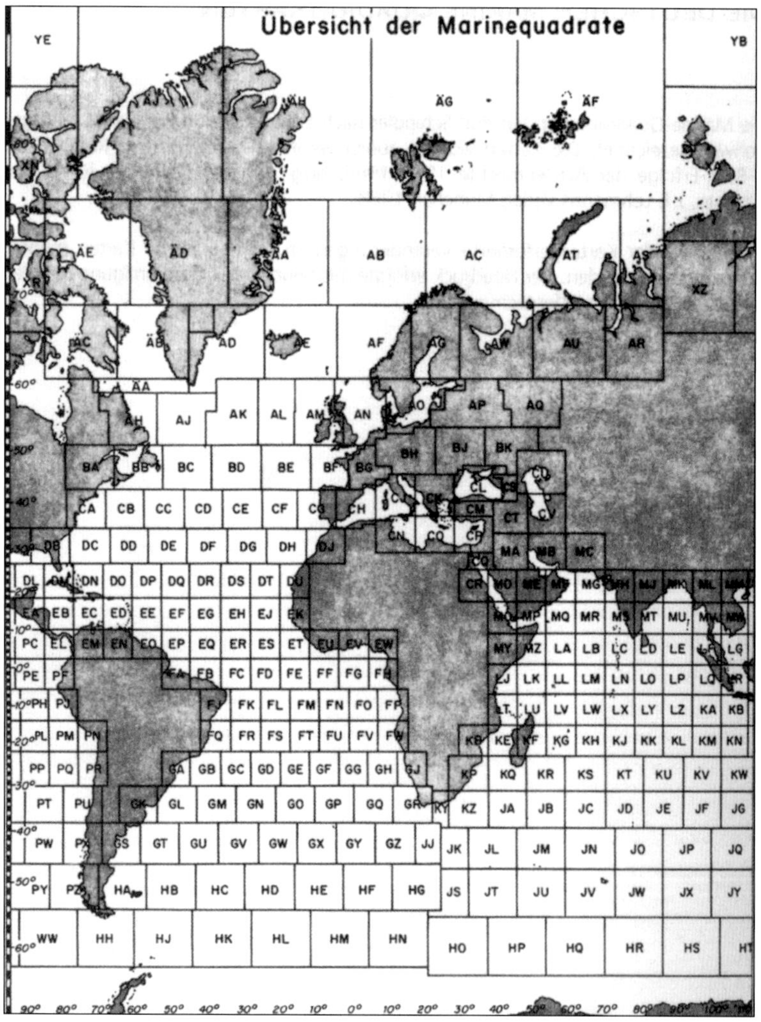


By dividing the Atlantic Ocean into squares, identified by two letters on a chart, it was possible for the German Navy to locate its ships. Each square is re-cut into eighty-one squares, themselves re-cut into another eighty-one squares. *LB*

# *October 1940: Departure of the IIC and VIIA-type U-boats*

OCTOBER 1940

| U-BOOT | TYPE | FLOT. | COMMANDER | ARRIVAL | DEPART | NOTES |
|---|---|---|---|---|---|---|
| **Present** | | | | | | |
| **U-28** | VIIA | 2 | Günter Kuhnke Future Chief of the 10th Flotilla | 5 | | Final departure turned into a school ship, relegated 4.8.44. Score: 14 ships sunk and 1 damaged |
| **U-47** | VIIB | 7 | Günther Prien Oak Leaves awarded the 20 October | 23 | 14 | |
| **U-48** | VIIB | 7 | Heinrich Bleichrodt | 5 | | Final departure, patrols out of St. Nazaire then turned into a school ship in June 41, scuttled 3.5.45. Score: 53 ships sunk and 4 damaged, U-boat with the highest number of ships sunk and for the highest tonnage |
| **U-58** | IIC | 1 | Heinrich Schonder | 2 | | Final departure, turned into a school ship, scuttled the 3.5.45. Score: 7 ships sunk and 1 damaged |
| **U-59** | IIC | 1 | Joachim Matz | 3 | | Final departure, turned into a school ship, scuttled the 3.5.45. Score: 16 ships sunk and 1 damaged, 1 submarine chaser and 1 minesweeper |
| **U-65** | IXB | 2 | Hans-Gerrit von Stockhausen | 15 | | Destination: Freetown sector! |
| **U-99** | VIIB | 7 | Otto Kretschmer | 22 | 13 \ 30 | |
| **U-100** | VIIB | 7 | Joachim Schepke | 23 | 12 | |
| **U-101** | VIIB | 7 | Fritz Frauenheim | 24 | 5 | Change of commander |
| **U-124** | IXB | 2 | Georg-Wilhelm Schulz | 5 | | |
| **U-137** | IID | 1 | Herbert Wohlfahrt | 17 | 9 | |
| **U-138** | IID | 1 | Wolfgang Lüth Knight's Cross awarded the 24 October | 19 | 8 | Change of commander |
| Arrivals | | | | | | |
| **U-29** | VIIA | 2 | Otto Schuhart | 1 | 26 | First arrival in Lorient, put into service 16.11.36; final departure, turned into a school ship, scuttled 4.5.45. Score: 11 ships sunk and 1 aircraft-carrier |
| **U-32** | VIIA | 2 | Hans Jenisch Knight's Cross awarded the next day | 6 | 24 | Final departure, scuttled 30.10.40 after being damaged by depth charges, 9 men killed and 33 saved, including the commander. First U-boat in Lorient lost during on operation. Score: 22 ships and 4 damaged |
| **U-31** | VIIA | 2 | Wilfried Prellberg | 8 | 19 | First arrival in Lorient, put into service 28.12.36; first time sunk by a plane, refloated and put back into service 31.7.40; final departure, sunk by depth charges the 2.11.40. 2 crewmembers killed, 43 captured. Only U-boat sunk twice by enemy action. Score: 10 ships sunk and 2 damaged |
| **U-43** | IXA | 2 | Wilhelm Ambrosius | 18 | | First arrival in Lorient, put into service 26.8.39; change of commander |
| **U-103** | IXB | 2 | Viktor Schütze | 19 | | First arrival in Lorient, put into service 5.7.40 |
| **U-37** | IXA | 2 | Viktor Oehrn Knight's Cross awarded on arrival | 22 | | Change of commander |
| **U-123** | IXB | 2 | Karl-Heinz Moehle | 23 | | First arrival à Lorient, put into service 30.5.40 |
| **U-38** | IXA | 2 | Heinrich Liebe | 24 | | Remained nearly two months in repairs |

*Movements*: fourteen arrivals, sixteen departures, number of U-boats present at the end of the month: ten.

*Observations*: The last four VIIA and IIC – type U-boats left Lorient definitively to be repatriated to Germany where they were turned into school ships. The time spent in the port receiving supplies and light repairs remained around fifteen days. It should be noted that a total of four U-boats left on September 5 because, according to the Commander of U-boat Operations' war diary, the weather had been so awful the day before that U-boats which had left that day had to turn back because the motorboats couldn't put out to sea to escort them. Doubtlessly, to relieve the congested port and give priority to the most active U-boats needing repairs, on September 5, U-28 VIIA-type was sent to St. Nazaire where it stayed for a week in dry dock; it was retired from service after a last weather-report patrol.

The first successful wolfpack attack during the Battle of the Atlantic, during which almost an entire convoy was destroyed, took place in mid-October: the SC-7 convoy was spotted by U-48 on October 17, and a line of U-boats was immediately formed with U-46, U-99, U-100, U-101 and U-123. The trap closed on the convoy, which crossed the line and then was attacked at 18:00 the same evening; it lost twenty-one ships and two other were damaged. The slaughter continued on October 19 and 20 against the HX-79 convoy where twelve merchant ships were sunk and two other damaged. In October 1940, U-boats results were 920 tons of enemy ships sunk per U-boat and per day at sea. These catastrophic numbers for the British were mainly due to the wolfpack attack on the SC-7 and HX-79 convoys, which the submariners nicknamed *"the night of the long knives."* For Britain, October

Somewhere between October 1 and 26, *Kapitänleutnant* Otto Schuhart (on the right) strolls round *Saltzwedel Kaserne* with a member of the 2nd Flotilla's ground personnel. The Knight's Cross was awarded to the commander of U-29 on May 16, 1940, for having sunk the aircraft carrier and 70,000 tons worth of merchant ships. *LB*

The day after his arrival in Lorient, Commander Hans Jenisch of U-32 is decorated with the Knight's Cross. *Bernd Siepert*

*Kapitänleutnant* Wilfried Prellberg, commander of U-31, which only called once in Lorient. This U-boat is the first to have attacked a convoy since the beginning of the war, on September 16, 1939. It is also the only U-boat to be sunk twice by the Allies! It had been sunk for the first time on March 11, 1940, just off Wilhelmshaven by an RAF plane during maintenance tests; all the crew on board and thirteen workmen from the shipyards were killed; the U-boat had been refloated, repaired, and put into service on July 31, 1940. Leaving Lorient on October 19, 1940, it was sunk a second time on November 2 by depth charges launched by the British destroyer *HMS Penelope*; this time, two of the crew were killed and forty-four survived. It was the second U-boat out of Lorient to be destroyed during a patrol. *UBA*

18 and 19, 1940, which saw the destruction of twenty-eight Allied ships, were some of the worst days of the Atlantic war.

In mid-October, the different German General Staff, met in Paris to prepare the invasion of England, decided to abandon the project. To be closer to the theatre of operations and the men, the U-boat Corps Command began to move its offices to the Kernével peninsula, in the Larmor-Plage district.

On October 15, U-65 was the first boat, after U-A in June, to be sent on a trial patrol in the South Atlantic, even though targets were still numerous in the North Atlantic. U-65 was re-supplied by the fuel tanker *Nordmark* off the Cape Verde Islands before sailing to Freetown. Out of Germany in October 1940, the *Nordmark* had accompanied the pocket battleship *Admiral Scheer* during its campaign in the South Atlantic and had stayed on to serve as a re-supply ship when the battleship returned to Germany in March 1941. U-65 sank eight ships during its patrol, including four fuel tankers, and damaged a fifth before returning to Lorient on January 10, 1941, at the end of a long patrol of nearly three months. Even if its results had been correct, when they were calculated in proportion to tonnage sunk per day at sea, they remained clearly inferior to the results obtained by other U-boats in the North Atlantic. Operations in this sector only restarted in January 1941 for U-37 and in February 1941 for three other U-boats.

In 1940, an exceptional decoration, Oak Leaves for the Knight's Cross, were awarded to three commanders who had theoretically passed the 200,000 tons of ships sunk. The first was Günther Prien, commander of U-47, who received this decoration on October 20, 1940, following his report of the destruction of eight ships representing 50,000 tons during his last patrol. In reality, by December 6, 1940, he had a total of twenty-seven ships sunk for 177,793 tons to his credit as well as numerous ships damaged in ten combat patrols since September 3, 1939. The number of 177,793 tons corresponded to ships effectively sunk. At the epoch, commanders couldn't always verify that the torpedoes having exploded on reaching their objective had really sunk the ship targeted or had just damaged it; sometimes even, two explosions were attributed to two different ships when in truth only one had been hit. Which was why the number of successes claimed was higher than the reality: thirty-nine ships sunk at the end of 1940 for Günther Prien. The second to receive Oak Leaves on November 4 was Otto Kretschmer, followed by Joachim Schepke on December 1. From October 23 to 30, the three Aces were reunited for the second and last time in Lorient. After a meal and plenty of wine to celebrate Prien's decoration, Schepke suggested a friendly bet: who would be the first to reach 250,000 tons of ships sunk? The loser would pay the champagne for the other two!

On October 20, 1940, *Vizeadmiral* Walter Matthiae was named as the new Chief of the German Navy War Shipyards in Lorient. French Mechanics Engineer 1st Class Le Puth was working in the arsenal at the epoch. In his memoirs he wrote: "*Rear-Admiral Matthiae was, they said, a*

On October 5, 1940, U-48 leaves Lorient for the last time for the Western Approaches, the area of sea that extends from the west coast of the British Isles to the 15E meridian line. This U-boat, whose insignia is a black cat with "3X" written between its paws, will carry out four more patrols before being turned into a U-boat school in the Baltic. With fifty-one cargo ships sunk representing 306,875 tons, one warship sunk, and three damaged ships, it ranked the highest success rate of all the U-boats during Second World War. It was scuttled off Neustad, Germany, on May 3, 1945. *UBA*

U-32 arrived in Lorient for the second time on October 6, 1940. A year earlier on October 18, 1939, the U-boat sank the British ship *Kensington Court,* whose thirty-four crewmembers were rescued by two *Sundrland* flying boats. This air-sea rescue by seaplane was the first realized during the Second World War. *LB*

Commander of the 2nd U-Flotilla, Fischer, makes his welcome speech the crew. On its next patrol, departing from Lorient on October 24, the U-32 will carry an additional officer who will be considered a sign of bad luck for the crew; this will indeed be the last operation of the U-32. On October 30; two days before disappearing, U-32 sank the 42,348 ton British steamer the *Empress of Britain. LB*

On the right bank of the Scorff, torpedoes are loaded on board an IX-type U-boat using a crane installed on a barge. *UBA*

On October 13, 1940, U-99 left for its fifth combat patrol, which was a success with the attack on the SC-7 convoy that resulted in twenty-one ships sunk and two damaged; for its part, U-99 sank six and damaged a seventh of them. Out of superstition, several crewmembers and in particular the navigator, Petersen, with Kretschmer since 1937, had insisted on changing the departure date as not to leave on the 13th. When far out to sea, they received a message from the U-boat Operations Command announcing that the port was closed because of mines placed by the British sometime during the previous night. They had passed them without knowing it! Just above the horseshoe insignia on the conning tower, is Commander Kretschmer. Very strict about rules, he is wearing the blue winter cap and not a white one as other commanders usually do, a practice however completely tolerated by the General Staff of the U-boat Corps to create team spirit. *LB*

Drivers of *NSKK-Hauttransportkolonne 8* have been granted permission to have a photo souvenir taken on U-47's rear bridge. The photo is hung on the fuel tankers' wharf. Like the U-boat crews, some of the drivers have recuperated British jackets, more practical than their large jackets. *LB*

This photograph of U-47's profile makes it possible to see the radio wire coming from the conning tower to connect to the antenna wire stretching from the conning tower to the front of the U-boat. The camouflage, using large-mesh nets and tarpaulin is very primitive. On the right: *Salztwedel Kaserne* buildings. *LB*

Günther Prien greets his comrades; he is carrying a briefcase containing directives from the General Staff, only to be opened once on board. As he had often flown from Valves Airport, Prien knew the pilots of the *KG 100* Squadron who "adopted" U-47. *LB*

Before his departure on October 14, 1940, Commander Prien is interviewed by war correspondent Kurt Esmarsch. *LB*

U-47 is sent on a weather-report patrol to the west of the British Isles. It is there that he spotted the HX-79 convoy five days after his departure. *LB*

**Above:** U-103 arrived in Lorient for the first time on October 19, 1940, and was docked near the old sloop-transport *Isere*. This U-boat, whose commander, Schütze, later became the new head of the 2nd U-Flotilla in August 1941, will give the fleet its emblem representing the rune of victory. This type IXB U-boat had an excellent first patrol, sinking a record of five ships. *LB*

**Left:** On October 18, 1940, U-43 arrived for the first time in Lorient, commanded by Wilhelm Ambrosius. Although this commander obtained certain results during his five preceding combat patrols, he was considered by Dönitz's staff as not being dynamic enough in his attacks. He was replaced on the IXA-type by Commander Wolfgang Lüth who proved reliable in this field aboard U-138 IID-type which arrived in Lorient the following day. U-43 had problems in the future: on November 9, it left the port but had to return almost immediately because of technical problems. It left again on November 10 but had to turn back the following day because it left an oil slick on the water – various defects were also discovered during deep diving tests. In Dönitz's logbook, it was noted that disadvantages of this kind were to be envisaged as long as operational tests weren't systematically carried out before the U-boats left the shipyards. U-43 was finally able leave Lorient on November 17. *UBA*

*retired ship's captain, Director of the Navy Library in Berlin when the War broke out. He wasn't a bad man; he was a marine above all. The French Navy never complained about him."* The 650 Germans who worked in the shipyards rubbed shoulders with the French workers to whom the *Kriegsmarine* had left a small part of the arsenal to work on the warships that were still in construction in mid-1940, under the direction of General Engineer Antoine. Those who worked in the *Kriegsmarinewerft* (Navy War Shipyard) were spread out in different workshops called "Ressorts": *Ressort I Ausrüstung* (deposit and supplies) had the same tasks as the Port Commander, but only in the arsenal zone. They supplied fuel to the U-boats and auxiliary ships, repaired the mooring posts, towed ships to these posts and gave assistance to any damaged ships when they arrived. For these patrols, they had twenty-one tugs, twenty-four motorboats, six floating cranes, thirty-nine supply ships and barges as well as 350 vehicles (cars, trucks, buses). The *Ressort II Artillerie* was made up of two services: *II M* that took care of vehicle and light weapons maintenance and *II T* a technical workshop for electrical installations; on the other hand, munitions supplies, apart from torpedoes, was ensured by the arsenal's Artillery Service in Lorient. *Ressort III Schiffbau* – (shipyards) worked on U-boat hulls, notably repairing damage caused by bad weather and Allied guns and depth charges; this service also removed any seaweed and shells that might have got attached during a patrol. *Ressort IV Machinenbau* (mechanical engineering) was made up of two main services: *IV U* maintenance of Diesel and electric engines and *IV E* electrical installations. *Ressort V Hafenbau* (harbor buildings) took care of any work in the port, on land, and in the water that were linked to the arsenal. *Ressort VI Navigation* was in charge of the Navy's entire equipment of nautical instruments, sea charts, log books, etc. and to their installation; they supplied chronometers, barographs, sextants, and spare parts for the gyroscopic and magnetic compasses and repeaters. *Ressort VII Torpedo* took care of the torpedoes and their loading in U-boats. *Ressort VIII Nachrichtenmittelbetrieb* (transmissions section) was in charge of the maintenance of radios aboard U-boats and all the other ships; this service ensured the installation of a huge telephone exchange for all the services in Lorient as well as the creation of a radio station with 16 high-powered transmitters so that from Kernével Dönitz's General Staff could communicate with U-boats on patrols. *K.M.W. Lorient* also had administration and health services, and staff, security and civil defense departments. ***Allied reactions***: On the aviation level: twelve British bombardments damaged the town and the port on October 7 and 28; these operations had limited means to hand: one to six planes each time; the arsenal zone was regularly hit. A total of four mine-laying patrols were carried out by four to six planes. On the maritime level: U-31 was attacked on October 8 by the British submarine *HMS Trident* in the Bay of Biscay while approaching Lorient; it launched two torpedoes at U-boat but missed; as the lookouts on U-31 thought they had seen the British submarine laying mines, a search was carried out. During its departure for Freetown on October 15, U-65 was attacked without success off Lorient by torpedoes from a British submarine. Before its first arrival in the port of Lorient on October 18, U-43 spotted the periscope of a British submarine. The next day, on October 19, U-31 found itself being the target of a failed attack by torpedoes from a British submarine. On October 21, following this increase in attacks by enemy submarines since August, *Vizeadmiral* Dönitz asked the *BdU* West to set up barriers to protect the approaches to Lorient from enemy submarines and mine-layers. ■

U-103 arrives in Lorient for the first time on October 19, 1940 – it is berthed alongside the old sloop-transporter *Isere*. This U-boat, whose Commander Schütze will become the new Chief of the 2nd Flotilla in August 1941 and will give the Flotilla its insignia representing the victory rune. This IXB-type carried out an excellent first patrol with five ships sunk. *LB*

Crewmen were always designated to perform guard duties around their U-boat during its arrival. Here the U-37 will remain for five weeks while in Lorient. *UBA*

On October 22 at 10:00, U-37 is back in Lorient with six pennants won to the west of the British Isles. *UBA*

Commander Viktor Oehrn of U-37 receives the Knight's Cross, with Prien on his left and Schepke on his right. Commander Oehrn will be taking a post on land with Dönitz's General Staff, where he worked before patrolling on U-37. *Charita*

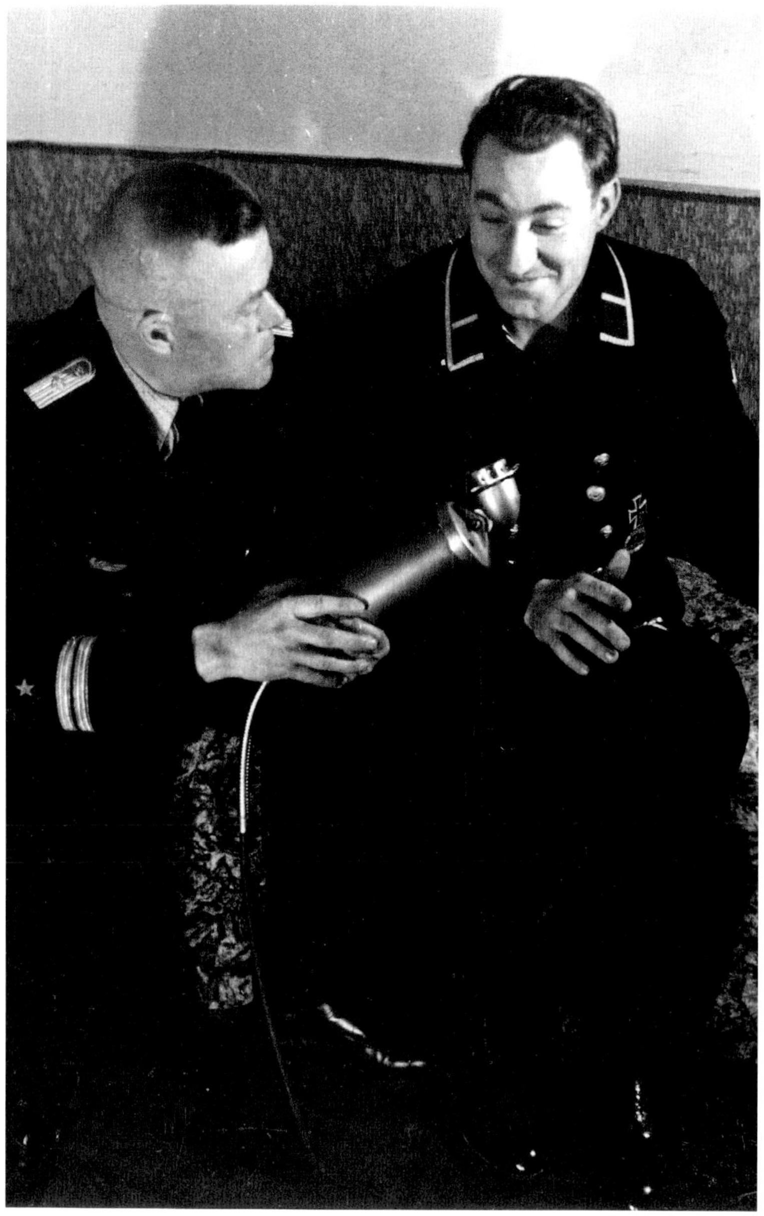

War correspondent *Oberleutnant* Kurt Esmarsch asks Josef Kassell, the radio operator on U-99, sent to the interview by Kretschmer, for details about their preceding patrol. *UBA*

Gerd Suhren, the Chief Engineer aboard U-37, is the first U-boat officer to receive the Knight's Cross on October 21, 1940, without being a commander. *Jean-Yves Nasse*

After the welcome ceremony, U-47 is moored on the left bank of the Scorff alongside the tankers' wharf. From here we can see the *Tour de la Découverte*. Prien talks to members of the shipyard about the details of the work needed on his U-boat. *UBA*

U-47 and U-100 side by side on the Scorff after their arrival. The logbook of U-100 gives the following details relating to its stay in the Lorient shipyards: "*October 23, 11:20: arrival and U-boat moored; 13:30: the U-boat is emptied, work has begun in the shipyard. October 26, 13:45: entry into the basin. October 28, 14:30: left the basin, moored in the east Scorff. November 4, 9:30: the U-boat leaves its position and berths on the Isere. November 5: equipping the U-boat, loading torpedoes and the diesel. November 6: loading provisions. November 7, 11:30: departure for the fourth patrol.*" *LB*

On October 26, 1940, U-29 left Lorient for a particular patrol: escorting the *Raider 21 Widder*. The U-boat was then repatriated to Germany to be used as a training U-boat for new crews. With this last departure, all the IIC and VIIA-type U-boats left Lorient for good. *Charita*

On October 24, 1940, three days after having left the command of U-138, Wolfgang Lüth was awarded the Knight's Cross. Even if he hadn't reached the 100,000 tons of Allied ships sunk, his successes on the two II-type U-boats justified the decoration, according to the U-boat Corps Command. It should be noted that during a patrol on U-9, Lüth had sunk the French submarine *Dory* in May 1940 and that he had sunk four ships in one night alone during his first patrol on U-138. He will be the only commander decorated with the Knight's Cross for tonnage sunk in a type-II U-boat. *Charita*

# November 1940: Admiral Dönitz Settles in Kernével

NOVEMBER 1940

| U-Boot | Type | Flot. | Commander | Arrival | Depart | Notes |
|---|---|---|---|---|---|---|
| Present | | | | | | |
| **U-37** | IXA | 2 | Nicolai Clausen | | 28 | New commander |
| **U-38** | IXA | 2 | Heinrich Liebe | | | Repairs |
| **U-43** | IXA | 2 | Wolfgang Lüth Former commander of U-138 | 9<br>11 | 9<br>10<br>17 | New commander; return to Lorient during the day with a leaking fuel tank, second departure the 10th return the 11th, third departure the 17th |
| **U-47** | VIIB | 7 | Günther Prien | | 3 | |
| **U-100** | VIIB | 7 | Joachim Schepke | 27 | 7 | |
| **U-101** | VIIB | 7 | Ernst Mengersen | | 24 | New commander |
| **U-103** | IXB | 2 | Viktor Schütze | | 9 | |
| **U-123** | IXB | 2 | Karl-Heinz Moehle | 28 | 14 | |
| **U-137** | IID | 1 | Herbert Wohlfahrt | | 3 | Final departure, a few patrols in Norway then turned into a school ship, scuttled 2.5.45. Score: 7 ships sunk, 2 damaged |
| **U-138** | IID | 1 | Peter Lohmeyer | | 5 | New commander |
| Arrival | | | | | | |
| **U-99** | VIIB | 7 | Otto Kretschmer | 8 | 27 | Destroyed two British auxiliary cruisers |
| **U-124** | IXB | 2 | Georg-Wilhelm Schulz | 13 | | |
| **U-93** | VIIC | 7 | Claus Korth | 29 | | First arrival in Lorient, put into service 30.7.40 |

Fifteen days after his brother Gerd Suhren, Chief Engineer on the U-37 (on the left), Reinhard "Teddy" Suhren, Watch Officer on U-48, receives the Knight's Cross on November 3, 1940. These brothers are the first officers of the *Kriegsmarine* to receive this decoration without being commanders. *Charita*

*Movements*: seven arrivals, twelve departures, number of U-boats present in Lorient at the end of the month: five.

*Observations*: The few arrivals didn't cover the number of departures and only one new U-boat put into Lorient. In November, to avoid the British escort ships which were reinforcing in the Western Approaches, U-boats had to reroute towards the west. They left the tenth to the fifteenth Meridian sector where ships had been numerous until then to set up west of the fifteenth Meridian. If this displacement was an advantage for the arrival of other U-boats around a convoy before it reached the British Isles, the sector to watch was vast and the convoys more difficult to find. In addition, the foul weather that settled in for the last two months of the year complicated attack conditions when a convoy was spotted. For example, on November 24, four convoys were sighted but the bad weather prevented a wolfpack attack. All of a sudden, U-boat success rates fell by more than half in relation to the previous month. In November 1940, U-boats didn't sink more than 430 tons of enemy cargo ships per day. During this month four U-boats put out of Lorient with a new commander. For example, U-43 IXA-type, whose commander had been considered not being daring enough by the General Staff; Lüth, the new commander, had proved himself by being decorated with the Knight's Cross gained with U-138, a IID-type coastal U-boat whose command was given to another officer. The commanders of the other two took posts on land: Oehrn was named 1st officer of the Admiral's General Staff in the department of the U-boat Corps Operations while Frauenheim was sent to the Baltic Sea as an instructor for U-boat officer candidates. On April 6, 1941, he returned to the region after being named Navy Liaison Officer to the Chief of Atlantic Aviation.

The U-93 was the first VIIC-type to arrive in a French port. Even though its characteristics were more-or-less the same as the VIIB, it had considerable improvements to become the model that Dönitz and his submariners had dreamed of. Measuring 67.1 meters long and 6.2 meters wide and with a displacement of 761 tons on the surface and 865 tons submerged, the VIIC had an action range of 6,500 miles on the surface at twelve knots. It had a top speed of seventeen knots on the surface and 7.6 submerged, which was a little slower than the VIIB due to its length while its engine power was the same. Like the VIIB, its armament was made up of five torpedo launching tubes, four in front and one in the back. It carried fourteen torpedoes like the VIIB, as well as its surface

The first soldier of the *Kriegsmarine* not being an officer to receive the Knight's Cross on November 5, 1940, was *Stabsobersteuermann* Heinrich Petersen, the navigator on U-99. He had accompanied Kretschmer during twelve patrols since the beginning of the war. *Charita*

On November 3, U-137 leaves Lorient for the last time. In the foreground is the conning tower of U-47, which will also be leaving the port. U-137 left for its fourth combat patrol taking it to Bergen in Norway! Turned into a U-boat school in January 1941, it returned to active service in June and July to support the German attack against the USSR. *UBA*

On November 3, Günther Prien inspects his crew before the departure of U-47 for its eleventh combat patrol to the west of the British Isles. In November, to avoid the British escort ships that were reinforced in the Western Approaches, Dönitz ordered his U-boats to move further west, past the fifteenth meridian line. *LB*

weapons. The main differences were in its interior equipment. The development of a new, high-performance objective detection device (*Such Gerät*) had been finished just before the construction of VIIC U-boats and the space for this equipment hadn't been planned for the VIIB. The VIIC received it simply because it was 60cm larger than its predecessor! This extra space increased the volume of the conning tower situated above the control room as well as the capacity of its tanks to 5.4m3, which allowed it to have the same action range as the VIIB in spite of its larger size. The mechanics had also been improved, notably the installation an oil-filtering system for the diesel engines in order to improve their service life. In addition, to economize on the electric engines, a diesel compressor had replaced one of the two electric compressors, used to refill the compressed-air tanks, for launching torpedoes, and filling the ballasts. Finally, the electric control system had been modernized.

Otto Kretschmer added Oak Leaves to his Knight's Cross on November 4, 1940. As commander of U-23 between October 4, 1939 and February 22, 1940, he had sunk eight ships totaling 27,624 tons. During his seven combat patrols from June 18 to December 12, 1940 as commander of U-99, he had a total of twenty-nine ships sunk for 182,947 tons and had damaged several other ships. Therefore, his score at the end of 1940 of thirty-seven ships sunk for 210,571 tons, made him the ace of U-boat Corps "Aces" during the entire Second World War.

According to the war diary of the Commander of the German U-boat Corps, it was on November 11, 1940 at 09:00 that his Operation Department was officially installed on the Kernével peninsula where three villas, *"Kérillon," "Margaret" and "Kerozen"* had been requisitioned, just opposite Kéroman. The first, which housed *Vizeadmiral* Dönitz, had been nicknamed by the submariners "the sardine chateau." Since the summer of 1940, the *Todt Organization had* been in charge of building three large bunkers to shelter General Staff and the radio equipment that kept it in contact with U-boats at sea. For this a long radio antenna had been set up in front of a small jetty on the peninsula. A ring of defensive bunkers protected access to the peninsula both by sea and land. From Kernével, *Vizeadmiral Dönitz* could efficiently organize his wolfpack tactics: when a U-boat sighted a convoy, it contacted Dönitz's command post by radio which then sent other U-boats to the location; the first U-boat tracked the convoy without attacking until the others arrived and then the group attack could start, which noticeably disorganized the British defense system. In order to react without delay to outside events, Dönitz organized debriefing meetings with each U-boat commander on his return from a patrol. The commander would forward his logbook that recorded everything that took place during the patrol as well as notes about future possible improvements, suggestions about the new material installed, etc. Dönitz would read the report and then pass it to *Fregattenkapitän* Eberhard Godt Chief of the Operations Department, before the meeting with the commander. Discussions were direct; Dönitz never hesitated to encourage his men to speak frankly. Once the meeting was over, Godt completed the commander's report by a personal assessment. All this information and the

On November 4, 1940, having reached 200,000 tons of ships sunk, Otto Kretschmer is the second U-boat commander to receive Oak Leaves for his Knight's Cross. *Charita*

During leave, accompanied by another member of the crew from U-100, *Obergefreiter* Wilhelm Schmidt (right), arrives in Nantes to see his brother (center) a train driver in the *Reichsbahn*. Wilhelm Schmidt was lucky to be one of the six survivors of U-100 when it was destroyed on March 17, 1941. *UBA*

Until the return of Prien at the beginning of December in Lorient, "Silent Otto" Kretschmer was the most decorated officer. However, he wasn't attracted by propaganda and carefully avoided interviews. From left to right: Heinz Fischer Chief of the 2nd Flotilla, *KL* Hugo Baehr the Flotilla's Chief of Police, Otto Kretschmer and *KK (MA)* Slickers of the Coastal Artillery, commander of the *M.A.A. 264. LB*

U-99 is put into dry dock in basin No.2 in the arsenal. *Bernd Siepert*

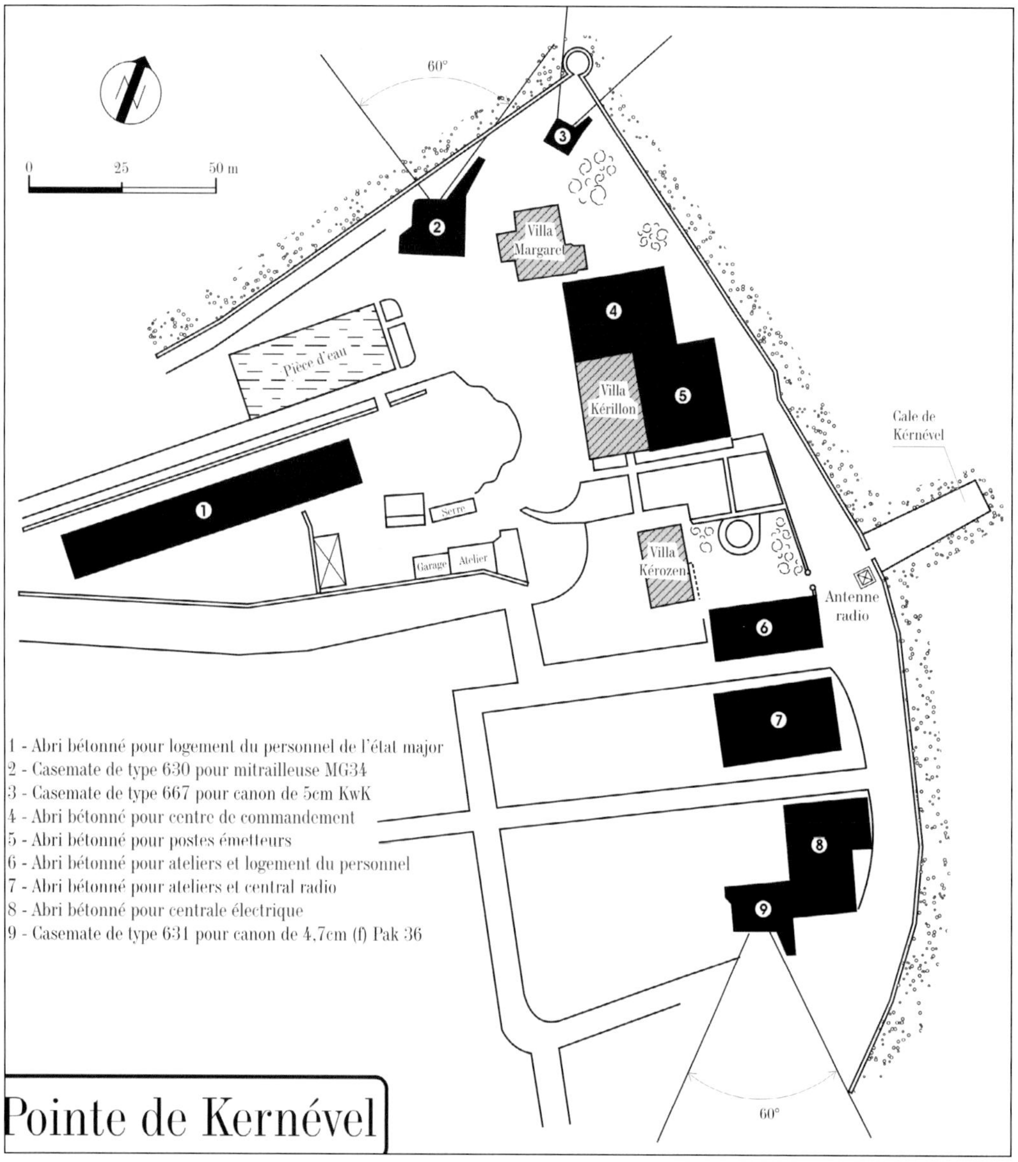

Appointed 1st officer of the Admiral's staff in Kernével the previous month, *Kapitänleutnant* Victor Oehrn assists the arrivals and departures of the U-boats as a spectator. *LB*

The victory rune insignia of U-103. When its commander, Viktor Schütze, is named Chief of the 2nd Flotilla during the summer of 1941, this emblem will be adopted by all the U-boats of this flotilla. *LB*

On the peninsula of Kernével, several members of Dönitz's staff drink a glass of champagne on *Margaret* Villa's balcony; in the center is Dönitz's personal pilot. *UBA*

suggestions that came directly from the field as it were, were duplicated in six copies intended for the following units: one copy for the *BdU* Operations Department; one for the *BdU* Organization Department; two for the *OKM* Direction of Naval Operations, one for the Flotilla and one that was kept aboard the U-boat. Thanks to this debriefing directly after the return from a patrol, improvements could be rapidly carried out on the U-boats and attack techniques improved. The General Staff of the U-boat Corps Direction of Operations in Kernével was operational 24/7.

All the daily information coming from the U-boats' radios were recorded on huge sea charts which covered the walls in the two operations rooms; copies of the information deciphered by *B-Dienst*, the German radio observation service, were also stored here. Pushpins and small flags symbolized

Bunkers on the point used to shelter transceivers are surmounted by antennas for long-distance communication with the U-boats at sea. *BA*

We can see the day periscope bent horizontally! Commander Karl-Heinz Moehle and his crew had been very lucky. *UBA*

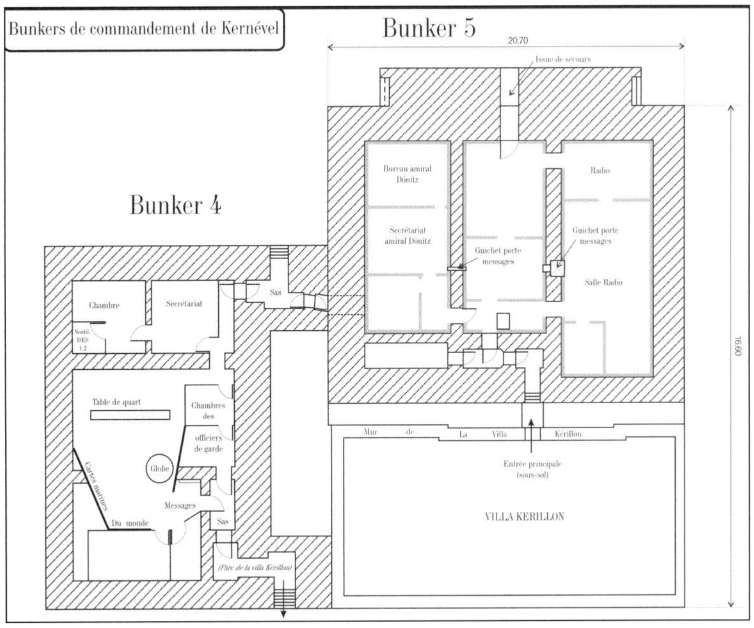

Admiral Dönitz had a Focke-Wulf Fw 200 *Condor* nicknamed "*Albatros*" at his disposal for displacements. It had the decoration obtained by submariners after three combat patrols painted on it. It was kept at Valves-Meucon Airfield. *DR*

On November 28, 1940, U-123 arrives in Lorient with a well-damaged conning tower. Its logbook noted that on November 23, after having sunk five ships in the OB-244 convoy between 04:16 and 09:14, while it was on the surface U-123 was attacked by artillery from an armed steamer at 09:45; the U-boat dived to 14m at 10:06 but this depth wasn't sufficient. At 10:32 it was rammed by a ship and was forced to dive to 30m. It only surfaced at 19:38 to find that its attack periscope had broken off and that the day periscope at been bent at a 90° angle! To fly its pennants, they had to cobble together an impromptu mast. *UBA*

Several commanders welcome their comrades; a workman from the shipyards wears the round badge of the arsenal in Wilhelmshaven on his garrison cap. *UBA*

Commander Moehle recounts his adventure. From left to right: Moehle, Herbert "*Vati*" Schultze, former commander of U-48 and interim Chief of the 7th Flotilla, and Joachim Schepke, commander of U-100. *LB*

A welcome committee has gathered to congratulate the crew of U-123 for returning unscathed from a lively patrol. *Charita*

On November 29, 1940, U-93 is the first VIIC-type to come in Lorient. Although it belongs to the 7th Flotilla, Commander Claus Korth is welcomed by *Korvettenkapitän* Fischer, Chief of the 2nd Flotilla. *Charita*

U-boats' positions, the convoys shipping lanes, the zones watched and the action range of the British planes. Other graphs noted weather conditions sector by sector, the direction of the sea currents and information about every U-boat in order to know how long it could stay in operation zones, etc. The important operation for Dönitz and his staff was to find zones where enemy traffic was dense and where the defenses were weakest; as soon as such a zone was attacked, the British reinforced their maritime and aerial escorts, so new zones had to be found each time. The Battle of the Atlantic was played like a chess game where the opponents placed and displaced their pieces. In Kernével, a third room called the "museum" inventoried all the known result since the beginning of the battle. A graph showed the tonnage sunk per U-boat per day.

On October 28, 1940, Dönitz met with Hitler in Paris, when the latter returned from his meeting with Franco in the Basque country. The commander of the U-boat Corps asked him to officially intervene as soon as possible with the *Todt Organization* to protect U-boats in the three French bases of Lorient, Brest and St. Nazaire. With this in mind, Dr. Fritz Todt arrived in Lorient on November 15 for a two-day visit. With *Vizeadmiral* Lindau, representing the Kriegsmarine High Command in France, *Konteradmiral* Siemens from the Direction of Navy Operations, and *Vizeadmiral* Dönitz, a program for the construction of U-boats bases was set up for the future: twelve U-boat shelters were planned for Lorient and Brest, eleven in St. Nazaire. Work on them started immediately.

***Allied reactions***: The British carried out seventeen bombing patrols on Lorient during November; the raids almost daily from the 7th to the 15th and the 19th to the 23rd. A part from the first raids carried out by twenty aircraft, the other patrols were carried out with less than ten. The zone targeted was the military arsenal, which was hit almost each time. In the report on the raid carried out in the night of November 22/23, the following observations were noted: "*Military port – explosions near the dry dock, the electric station and the forges – two crewmembers confirmed seeing three explosions near the dry dock, south of Caudan bridge and the workshops near the west bank of the Scorff – other explosions near the U-boat base under construction on the east bank of Scorff.*" This report confirms the beginning of earth-moving work for the small U-boat base on the Scorff. In addition, four more-or-less successful mine laying operations were carried out by three Hampden planes. A British submarine off Lorient carried out a last operation during November: on the 25th, *HMS Talisman* hailed the French fishing boat *Le Clipper* and sent it off Bordeaux to spy on U-boat movements in the sector before accompanying it to Falmouth. ■

## *December 1940: Only Four Patrols out of Lorient*

DECEMBER 1940

| U-BOOT | TYPE | FLOT. | COMMANDER | ARRIVAL | DEPART | NOTES |
|---|---|---|---|---|---|---|
| Present | | | | | | |
| **U-38** | IXA | 2 | Heinrich Liebe | | 18 | Arrived October 24, nearly two months in Lorient |
| **U-93** | VIIC | 7 | Claus Korth | | | Damaged during British bombardment on Lorient in the night of December 9/10 |
| **U-100** | VIIB | 7 | Joachim Schepke Awarded Oak Leaves the day before his departure | | 2 | Final departure, sunk after being rammed by destroyer the night of March 15/16, 1941, 38 dead including the commander, 6 survivors. Score: 26 ships sunk; 6 damaged |
| **U-123** | IXB | 2 | Karl-Heinz Moehle | | | Damaged during British bombardment on Lorient in the night of December 9/10 |
| **U-124** | IXB | 2 | Georg-Wilhelm Schulz | | 16 | |
| Arrival | | | | | | |
| **U-47** | VIIB | 7 | Günther Prien | 6 | | |
| **U-95** | VIIC | 7 | Gerd Schreiber | 6 | 16 | First arrival in Lorient, put into service 31.8.40 |
| **U-101** | VIIB | 7 | Ernst Mengersen | 7 | | |
| **U-99** | VIIB | 7 | Otto Kretschmer | 12 | | |
| **U-103** | IXB | 2 | Viktor Schütze Knight's Cross awarded on arrival | 12 | | |
| **U-43** | IXA | 2 | Wolfgang Lüth | 17 | | |
| **U-52** | VIIB | 7 | Otto Salman | 28 | | |
| **U-96** | VIIC | 7 | Heinrich Lehmann-Willenbrock | 29 | | First arrival in Lorient, put into service 14.9.40 |
| **U-94** | VIIC | 7 | Herbert Küppisch | 31 | | First arrival in Lorient, put into service 10.8.40 |

***Movements***: nine arrivals, four departures, number of U-boats present in Lorient at the end of the month: ten.

***Observations***: During the month of December 1940, only four U-boats put out of Lorient and the other bases in France weren't operational yet. This low number is an indication of the small resources available to the German U-boat Corps; as there was a delay while U-boats arrive at and leave their combat zone, Germany was fighting the most powerful naval force in the world with vastly reduced means. The small number of U-boats leaving on operations was doubled during January and February. Of the fourteen U-boats that passed through Lorient in December, nine belonged to the 7th Flotilla which was being transferred to St. Nazaire. The bad weather in the Atlantic and the small number of U-boats available continued to give the advantage to the British in relation to previous months. A single convoy was intercepted on December 1, by U-47, U-52, U-94, U-95, U-99 and U-101; the HX-90 lost ten ships and two others were damaged.

On December 1, 1940, Joachim Schepke adds Oak Leaves to his Knight's Cross. He sank two ships for 2,348 tons between September 30 and October 1, 1939 as commander of U-3; nine ships totaling 15,715 tons between January 9 and March 20, 1940, as commander of U-19; 26 ships totaling 137,765 tons in five combat patrols from August 9 to December 31, forty as commander of U-100; his score at the end of 1940 was really thirty-seven ships sunk for 155,828 tons. He was nicknamed "*Ihrer Majestät bestaussehender Offizier*" – "His Majesty's Best Looking Officer." U-100 left Lorient for the last time on December 2 for Germany where the crew was given ten weeks' leave. *LB*

U-47 arrived in Lorient for the third time on December 6, 1940, returning from its eleventh combat patrol. It took part in the only wolfpack attack on a convoy during December. However, the patrol didn't go smoothly: U-47, which sank a ship on the HX-90 convoy, abruptly plunged to 120m before the Chief Engineer could stabilize it. Brought into service in December 1938, it needed a complete overhaul in Lorient. The welcome was less ceremonial than it was when great successes were announced. Prien was welcomed by Werner Winter, 5th Officer of Dönitz's General Staff. *LB*

The day before his departure on December 1, Commander Schepke of U-100 added Oak Leaves to his Knight's Cross. Like Prien and Kretschmer, he had become famous throughout Germany. His score was impressive: in ninety days he had sunk twenty-three ships, which put him in first place for the number of ships destroyed during the month. It should be noted that this decoration hadn't been awarded at sea after his report of tonnage sunk, but only four days after his arrival in Lorient on November 27; the General Staff had obviously wanted to verify his report because Schepke was known to exaggerate his successes a little. He had difficulty clearly identifying the ships he declared to have sunk, so they were often noted in his logbook as over 10,000 tons. Like Prien before him, he had published a book in the autumn about his adventures to encourage young men to join the U-boat corps. The title was *U-Bootfahrer von heute* (*Submariners of Today*); he had drawn the twelve illustrations in the book himself. Of the three Aces, Schepke took the most active part in propaganda, above all during the ten weeks of leave that were granted to him after his arrival in Kiel on January 1, 1941. Notably, he made a great speech that was broadcast in the huge Berlin Sports Center Palais in February 1941.

On December 6, U-47 under Günther Prien put into Lorient; this time it didn't return with exceptional results with only one ship sunk and a fuel tanker damaged. His eleventh combat patrol hadn't gone as well as his others: his U-boat, a VIIB put into service in December 1938, was starting to get old. Three weeks after leaving Lorient on November 3, U-47 had sighted a convoy and waited until the other U-boats to attack in a pack. Not only had his torpedoes missed their target due to a problem with the firing system, but U-47, which had had to crash-dive faced with a destroyer, had descended to 120 meters before the crew could redress the situation. On November 20, Prien sent a radio message asking permission to return to Lorient for a complete overhaul of his U-boat. However, on the way back on December 2, the numerous problems hadn't prevented him from firing two torpedoes at two ships in a convoy signaled by U-101. On their arrival in Lorient, U-47's crew was lodged at *Saltzwedel Kaserne*

Using tugs from the shipyard, a VIIB-type U-boat is installed in the basin No.2 in the arsenal. *UBA*

A rare photo of Otto Kretschmer with a short beard; normally a stickler for discipline, he always made his men shave before arriving at the port. Admiral Dönitz will try to convince him to take a post on land too, but in vain. *UBA*

On December 12, 1940, at 17:15, U-103 arrives in Lorient where the brass band of the *211th Infantry Division* is waiting for it in front of the barracks. *LB*

Viktor Schütze, Commander of U-103, received a radio message the day before announcing that he had won the Knight's Cross, which he received in the port during the welcome ceremony. At the time, he is wearing a *Kriegsmarine* dishtowel as a scarf! *UBA*

During its stay in the shipyards, U-103 carries out a test-dive off the fishing port. In the distance is Kernével Point. *UBA*

Four crewmembers of U-103 take a break in front of one of the two personnel bunkers in *Saltzwedel Kaserne*. From left to right: Baumann, Alfons Karg, Alfred Behlau, Hagemeyer. *Benoit Senne*

and Prien in the Maritime Prefecture, where he arrived at the end of the day, after giving his report to Dönitz in Kernével. During the evening while walking round his U-47 in the arsenal, he encountered his Watch Officer, Amelung Von Varendorff, who had just been chosen for a training course that would make him the commander of another U-boat. Prien said that apart from a few sailors, he was the last of his men who had accompanied him since the beginning, all the others having been transferred to new U-boats so that others could profit from their experience. Prien said to his former officer: *"The next time, Daddy will be leaving with a new garden of children!"* A six-week repairs program for U-47 was planned, so the men were on leave for Christmas. As Prien's departure had been planned for December 12, he was summoned by Dönitz for a meeting in Kernével. Dönitz offered him a position on land as the instructor in a school, but Prien refuse; he preferred to continue the battle on the seas and take the command of a new U-boat. Dönitz accepted his decision and asked him to do just one last patrol on U-47 when it was repaired: take it to Germany where it would be turned into a school ship.

On December 12, U-99 put into Lorient for a complete overhaul that lasted over six weeks. Its commander, Otto Kretschmer gave his men three weeks leave and gave them the choice: stay in the region and in the sea resorts in Quiberon or Carnac, or accompany him skiing in Silesia – they could even bring their girlfriends along if they wanted. The evening after his arrival in the port, Kretschmer was invited to dine with the commander of the U-boat Corps in Kernével. All the commanders, used to the profusion of food when they returned from a patrol, found these meals a real drag because the admiral made it a point of honor not to serve at his table more than the rations authorized to the civilians in Germany! Having to go to Cologne the next day, Dönitz, who obviously had something in mind, suggested that Kretschmer accompany him in his car: the Admiral wanted to use the trip to convince the man he affectionately called *"my best student"* to take a post on land. But Kretschmer, who had been at sea since the beginning of the war, refused the proposition. While at the ski resort in the mountains, a German editor asked him to publish his memoirs as Prien and Schepke had, but Kretschmer, who was a very discreet man, didn't want to. He said he would only do so if Dönitz ordered him to! The editor told him that people in high places really wanted him to write a book to encourage young men to enlist in the U-boat corps. Due to a misunderstanding by the General Staff of Dönitz, who always stood by his commanders, the order to write the book was issued! So Kretschmer was interviewed by a ghost

On December 17, Wolfgang Lüth, commander of U-43, is welcomed by Heinz Fischer, Chief of the 2nd Flotilla. During his first patrol that lasted a little more than a month, aboard this U-boat, he sank three ships and damaged a fourth. *Bernd Siepert*

Work is being done on the Scorff on U-123's badly damaged conning tower, whose bent periscope has been straightened a little. A wooden scaffold has been set up around the conning tower to work on repairs. *LB*

writer sent by the editor, but he only gave short and precise answers when questioned about his patrols.

On December 24, *Großadmiral* Raeder, Commander-in-Chief of the Kriegsmarine, addressed the following Christmas greeting to his men: "*To all! Proud of its great successes, of its Army, the great German Empire celebrates its second Christmas at war. My sincere Christmas greetings go to all the men of the War Navy who, at their posts, have participated in the success and in the efficiency of our corps. In particular, I would like to thank all the brave crewmembers of our warships who are at sea today and who are celebrating Christmas on board, either facing the enemy or patrolling our coasts. To all I wish a particularly good holiday, a victorious patrol and a safe return.*"

On December 29, U-96 put into Lorient. Its commander, Kapitänleutnant Heinrich Lehmann-Willenbrock, carefully noted in his logbook all the details of the following days right down to where his men would be spending New Year's Eve: "*29.12: 16:13, berthed alongside the* Audacieuse, *welcomed by Korvettenkapitän Fischer, Chief of the Flotilla. 30.12: 09:00 – 11:30, unloading foodstuff and torpedoes, taken care of by the shipyards and maintenance program planned. 13:30 – 16:00 work in the shipyards, demagnetized (so that we don't attract magnetic mines). 31.12: 09:00, meeting with the General Staff. 15:00 Flotilla Chief Fischer hands out Iron Crosses: 2 Iron Crosses 1st Class and 17 2nd Class. 16:00,* departure *of the crew in a bus for Carnac for New Year's Eve. 1.1.41: Holiday. 2.1.41: U-96 Displaced by tugs and berthed in the arsenal next to U-52. 16:00, U-boat War Badge* awarded *to five crewmembers. 3.1: work in the shipyards, fuel taken care of. 4.1: 09:00, put into dry dock. 6.1: 10:30, taken out of dry dock for loading supplies. 7.1: loading tinned food, a submariner disembarked, two others affected to U-96. 8.1: loading fresh food and torpedoes. 17:31: displaced and berthed alongside the* Audacieuse; *Kapitänleutnant Dommes affected on board for his apprenticeship. 9.1: loading personnel's equipment, 15:00 good luck speech by the Chief of the Flotilla. 15:05:* departure. *15:50 accompanied by an escort to Point 2. 18:15, alert exercise, dived to fifty meters.*"

***Allied reactions***: The Royal Air Force increased the pressure on the port in Lorient in December by carrying out twenty bombing patrols with at least ten planes each time. During the British air attack in the evening of December 9, 1940, bombs hit the docks and damaged the U-boats U-123 and U-93, as well as a dock door. Due to this, work on these U-boats was extended. It was the first impact on a dock and the first time that U-boats in the port in Lorient were damaged, even though there had already been eighty-eight air raids. *Kapitänleutnant* Korth, commander of U-93, noted in his logbook: "*29.11: 14:40, Groix Island lighthouse in view at a distance of ten miles. 15:20 escorted by two patrol boats from Point 2. 16:46 the escorts leave. 17:17 arrival in Lorient in the arsenal and berthed alongside the* Isère. *30.11, displaced and berthed at the goods wharf, torpedoes unloaded. Displaced and berthed alongside the Surveillante. 1.12: moved from* the *Surveillante because the water isn't deep enough and berthed alongside the* Audacieuse. *Debriefing with the* BdU. *2.12,* departure *of those on leave, debriefing avec the Flotilla. 3-4.12, work in the shipyards*

Arriving in Lorient on December 29 after his first patrol, Commander Heinrich Lehmann-Willenbrock of U-96, claimed to have sunk 40,900 tons and to have damaged another ship of 10,700 tons; this was immediately noted by the Command which wrote in its logbook that he had acted in a coolheaded and decisive manner. The crewmembers gather round their Chief on New Year's Day spent in the *Grand Hotel* in Carnac. *UBA*

Arriving Lorient on December 28, 1940; *Kapitänleutnant* Otto Salman was the commander of U-52. His score was thirteen boats sunk and one damaged. In May 1941, U-52 was turned into a U-boat school in the Baltic, while Commander Salman was named 5th Officer of the U-boat Corps Command's General Staff. On May 2, 1945, with Admiral von Friedenburg, chief of the U-boat Corps' Organization Department based in Germany for the entire war, Salman was decorated with the Knight's Cross of the War Merit Cross with Swords. *LB*

U-94's insignia represents a ferocious fish biting the tail of the British lion. *LB*

The logbook belonging to *Kapitänleutnant* Kuppisch, commander of U-94, which arrived in Lorient on December 31 returning from its first patrol, testifies to the bad weather reigning in the Atlantic: "*10:30 31.12: Point 2 in sight; arrival in Lorient under escort; berthing on the 'Isere'; end of the patrol. The patrol was considerably disturbed by the bad weather. In over thirty-three days spent in the operation zone, the use of weapons was impossible for fifteen days because of the bad weather and during five other days we could only use them for a few hours during the day; however there were no problems with the personnel or the material; the crew was completely ready for combat.*" In his logbook, Commander Kuppisch states to have sunk four ships totaling 24,340 tons between December 2 and 11; in reality he sank three ships totaling 18,053 tons. His first patrol was very favorably commented on by Godt, Chief of the Operations Department of the *BdU*. *LB*

*5.12 9:30, put in basin No.2; 6-8.12, work in the shipyards; 9.12: during the air raid three bombs hit the basin level with the U-boat; the men on guard duty, who had taken refuge in a shelter until the end of the raid, reported that the hull had been badly damaged in six different places and in all it had been hit by 130 pieces of shrapnel; 10-11.12: waterproofing redone; 12.12: pressure testing and taken out of basin No.2.*" U-93 was put into basin No.1 on December 16 where work was carried out until January 3. After carrying out a test dive at sea near Point 2, and testing the different weapons on January 7, 1941, U-93 left Lorient on January 11, so finally the shrapnel hadn't delayed it much.

On Sunday, December 22, during the public funerals held for the British pilots killed when their *Hampden* crashed near the town two days earlier, numerous French civilians from Lanester arrived to express their sympathy. The local newspaper "*Nouvelliste du Morbihan*" covered the event: "*The funerals of the crewmembers killed on Friday morning, December 20, took place on Sunday morning in Lanester. Honors were presented by a section of the German Army. The officer in charge of the ceremony spoke, saluting the British pilots killed in the course of their duty as soldiers. Then, in accordance with German Army custom, a triple salvo was fired over the graves where the British pilots now rest. Among the gathering, apart from representatives of the German Army, we noted the presence of Mr. Rogel, Mayor of Lanester. Numerous residents of the town joined these personalities in an ultimate homage, as a gesture of respect to the memory these soldiers who died for their country.*" Since the beginning of the previous month the British forces had stopped their attacks against U-boats approaching Lorient, and only carried out a single mine-laying operation at the entrance to the port. ■

## *Summing Up the Situation in Battle of the Atlantic, 1940*

In 1940, the Allies lost 1,059 ships totaling 3,991,641 tons. Over half of these losses were due to U-boat action, the rest were split between the aviation, mines, the arrival of armed merchant ships, and finally fast motorboats. However, the British, who had only been able to build a million tons of ships for losses four times as important and whose naval repairs workshops were congested by 2½ million tons of damaged ships, were already re-organizing their defense. U-boats "Happy Days" in the Western Approaches were coming to an end. However, Dönitz, with the numbers to hand, told himself that anything was possible. A total of sixty-two U-boats were put into service since the beginning of the war while only thirty-three had been destroyed during operations. He estimated that the Allied construction possibilities were 200,000 tons a month, yet only a few dozen U-boats had been destroyed. And he was waiting for numerous new U-boats for 1941, almost the double with 120 units planned.

From July to December 1940, a total of forty-one U-boats had been put into service: twelve IID-types, four VIIB-types, twelve VIIC-types, nine IXB-types and four foreign submarines captured. For the first time since the beginning of the war, these putting into service largely surpassed the losses that equaled eight units for the same period. That being said, considering the average duration of three months of exercise, few would take part in the battle until 1941. With a third of those operational in the ports and the rest either heading to or returning from operation zones, there were hardly more than seven or eight U-boats on operation at the same time until the end of the year, which represented only 350 men in a combat zone! However, the number of U-boats increased progressively during the following months during which about ten units were put into service each month.

In fact, Dönitz completely underestimated the capacities of the American shipyards. In July 1940, the U.S. Congress voted finance for a warship construction program; it planned to put into service 1,325,000 tons in two years, the equivalent of the powerful Royal Navy in 1939! Nor could Dönitz, the British reactions would make the tasks of his commanders even more difficult, notably their considerable progress in the deciphering field. ■

# JANUARY – JUNE 1941: THE BRITISH GROW STRONGER

## *January 1941: Dönitz is Given Aircraft for Reconnaissance*

JANUARY 1941

| U-BOOT | TYPE | FLOT. | COMMANDER | ARRIVAL | DEPART | NOTES |
|---|---|---|---|---|---|---|
| Present | | | | | | |
| **U-43** | IXA | 2 | Wolfgang Lüth | | | First month of repairs |
| **U-47** | VIIB | 7 | Günther Prien | | | |
| **U-52** | VIIB | 7 | Otto Salman | | 22 | |
| **U-93** | VIIC | 7 | Claus Korth | | 11 | Arrived on November 29: one and a half months of repairs |
| **U-94** | VIIC | 7 | Herbert Küppisch | | 9 | |
| **U-96** | VIIC | 7 | Heinrich Lehmann-Willenbrock | 22 | 9<br>30 | Final departure the 30th; numerous patrols out of St. Nazaire, turned into a school ship in February 1943, destroyed during American bombardment 30.3.45. Score: 28 ships sunk and 4 damaged |
| **U-99** | VIIB | 7 | Otto Kretschmer | | | |
| **U-101** | VIIB | 7 | Ernst Mengersen | | 23 | |
| **U-103** | IXB | 2 | Viktor Schütze | | 21 | |
| **U-123** | IXB | 2 | Karl-Heinz Moehle | | 14 | Arrived on November 28: one and a half months of repairs |
| Arrival | | | | | | |
| **U-37** | IXA | 2 | Nicolaï Clausen | 7 | | Destination South Atlantic |
| **U-65** | IXB | 2 | Hans-Gerrit von Stockhausen Knight's Cross awarded the 14th | 10 | | U-65 kept for repairs until 12.4.41 |
| **U-95** | VIIC | 7 | Gerd Schreiber | 14 | | |
| **U-38** | IXA | 2 | Heinrich Liebe | 22 | | |
| **U-124** | IXB | 2 | Georg-Wilhelm Schulz | 22 | | |
| **U-105** | IXB | 2 | Georg Schewe | 31 | | First time in Lorient, put into service 10.9.40 |

During his departure from Lorient on January 9, 1941, Commander Heinrich Lehmann-Willenbrock aboard U-96 is greeted by Commander Nicolai Clausen of U-37. When Lehmann-Willenbrock is named Chief of the 9th Flotilla in Brest on May 1, 1942, the smiling sawfish insignia on his cap will be adopted by all the boats of the flotilla. *UBA*

On January 4, 1941, U-96 is put into dry dock in basin No.2 in the Lorient arsenal. *Pierre-Marie Rousseau*

U-96 leaves Lorient for the North Atlantic. During this second patrol, it sunk two large steamers: *Oropesa* and *Almeda Star*, each totaling more than 14,000 tons, which were travelling unescorted. This U-boat was used as a model by war correspondent Lothar-Günther Buchheim when he wrote the novel *Das Boot*, which later became a famous German film. *UBA*

On January 11 at 15:10, U-93 leaves for its third combat patrol. The 88mm, mostly used in the first months of the war to sink boats already damaged by a torpedo, will no longer be assembled aboard VIIC-type U-boats; the omnipresence of Allied planes will stop the U-boats from being able to surface in an attack zone. U-93 sank three ships in the SC-19 convoy and damaged a straggler of the SC-20 before being attacked in its turn by a *Whitley* plane, which forced it to turn back towards Lorient. *UBA*

In January 1941, the crewmembers of U-103 pose for a photo on the Scorff. On the right is basin No.2's door. During its preceding patrol in December, U-103 sank the British troop transporter *Calabria* that had been transporting Indian soldiers to England; 450 of them lost their lives. *UBA*

Four days after his arrival in Lorient on January 10, 1941, *Korvettenkapitän* Hans-Gerrit von Stockhausen was awarded the Knight's Cross. He had returned from a rather successful patrol of almost three months in the South Atlantic where U-65 sank eight ships including four tankers. Having left on October 15, 1940, it was the first U-boat sent from Lorient to this sector. *LB*

The crewmembers of U-100 take advantage of their ten-week leave in Germany to promote the values of the U-boat Corps. They are offered a week in Ruhpolding ski resort in Upper-Bavaria. *Oberfeldwebel* Weidinger of the *Mountain Jäger Regiment 100*, U-100's "twin Unit," gives skiing lessons to Wilhelm Schmidt and Robert Wehrschuhn. The former of these two young men was to become one of the six survivors of U-100 picked up by the British in March; the latter, who didn't go on U-100's last patrol, was later transferred to U-354. *UBA*

On January 11, 1941, Commander Claus Korth of U-93 says goodbye to his comrades in Lorient. U-93's stay in the arsenal had been prolonged to repair damage caused to the U-boat's hull during the British bombardment on December 9, 1940. *UBA*

U-93, whose insignia was a red devil catching Churchill in a net. *UBA*

It is the turn of the *Mountain Jäger Regiment 100* to be invited on board U-100. From left to right: Anton Plenk, famous cross-country skier, Schepke, and *Oberfeldwebel* Weidinger. *UBA*

***Movements***: seven arrivals, eight departures, number of U-boats present in Lorient at the end of the month: nine.

***Observations***: Half of the U-boats present in Lorient in January 1941 belonged to the 2nd Flotilla, the other half to the 7th Flotilla, which was soon to be transferred to St. Nazaire. Only one new U-boat put into Lorient at the end of the month, U-105. The duration of stay was extended to a month on average.

On December 14, 1940, Dönitz sent a note to the Navy Command asking for air reconnaissance over the Atlantic in order to guide his U-boats to convoys. The truth was that U-boats' observation means were very limited and when no convoy was sighted, they remained inactive; if long-range planes could take over this part of their work, results would be much better. On January 2, after a visit to *Großadmiral* Raeder Commander-in-Chief of the German Navy, *Vizeadmiral* Dönitz met with *General* Jodl in Berlin. The discussions centered on the demands of the U-boat Corps for aerial support in the shape of twelve long-range planes to ensure tactical patrols and reconnaissance. Following these talks, on January 7, 1941, Focke-Wulf Fw 200 *Condor* long-range planes belonging to the *KG 40*, the 1st Group of the Combat Squadron based in Bordeaux, were made available to the *Marine-Gruppe West* – German Navy Command in the West. Of the fourteen planes, half of them were operational for air reconnaissance in the Atlantic up to the twentieth meridian west, by flying from Bordeaux to Stavanger in Norway: they would guide U-boats towards convoys. The bombers also sank several ships whenever they could, but the rather imprecise information given by the pilots meant that cooperation between them didn't work well, unless the U-boats were very close to the objective signaled; often a convoy spotted by the planes during the day changed course and couldn't be found by the U-boats the following night. As Goering insisted that *"everything that flies"* belonged to him, on February 28, 1941, this squadron returned to the command of the *Luftwaffe*. In fact, a new post was specially created: Chief of Atlantic Aviation. Its General Staff settled near Lorient, in Chateau Brandérion. Its commander, named on March 31, 1941, was *Oberstleutnant* Martin Harlinghausen. This former marine, who had served in the *Reichsmarine* from 1923 to 1933 before becoming a pilot in the *Luftwaffe*, was often seen with Dönitz in Kernével. A post of Chief of Aviation North was also created in Stavanger in Norway. The biggest successes in this aviation/U-boat cooperation came in the summer of 1941 during attacks on convoys out of Gibraltar; at the beginning of the following year, the group *I /KG 40* was sent to Norway.

***Allied reactions***: Following the arrival in Brest of the heavy cruiser *Admiral Hipper* on December 27, 1940, bombardments were concentrated on this port and became less frequent on Lorient. The British only carried out three raids on Lorient during January 1941, with less than five planes each time. On the other hand, six mine-laying operations were carried out off the port. To counter British aviation, two anti-aircraft Navy battalions, the 704 and the 806, put together in Germany respectively in Kiel and Wilhelmshaven in mid-November 1940, arrived in Lorient in January; they were reinforced in April by the 807th Battalion from Cuxhaven. ■

# February 1941: Three U-boats Sent to the South Atlantic

FEBRUARY 1941

| U-BOOT | TYPE | FLOT. | COMMANDER | ARRIVAL | DEPART | NOTES |
|---|---|---|---|---|---|---|
| Present | | | | | | |
| **U-37** | IXA | 2 | Nicolai Clausen | 18 | 3 27 | Final departure from Lorient the 27th, turned into a school ship, scuttled 5.5.45. Score: 51 ships sunk and 1 damaged |
| **U-38** | IXA | 2 | Heinrich Liebe | | | |
| **U-43** | IXA | 2 | Wolfgang Lüth | | | After its second month in Lorient, U-43 was victim of a technical accident on February 4; it sank because of negligence, refloated but kept for repairs until 11.05.41 |
| **U-47** | VIIB | 7 | Günther Prien | | 20 | Final departure |
| **U-65** | IXB | 2 | Hans-Gerrit von Stockhausen | | | First month of repairs which lasted to 12.4.41 |
| **U-95** | VIIC | 7 | Gerd Schreiber | | 16 | |
| **U-99** | VIIB | 7 | Otto Kretschmer | | 22 | Final departure |
| **U-105** | IXB | 2 | Georg Schewe | | 22 | Departure a long patrol in the South Atlantic until June 13, third place on patrols rating with 12 ships sunk without putting into port |
| **U-124** | IXB | 2 | Georg-Wilhelm Schulz | | 23 | Departure for the South Atlantic |
| Arrival | | | | | | |
| **U-106** | IXB | 2 | Jürgen Oesten | 10 | 26 | First arrival à Lorient, put into service 24.9.40 – Departure for the South Atlantic |
| **U-93** | VIIC | 7 | Claus Korth | 14 | | Damaged during an air raid on February 11, repairs needed |
| **U-94** | VIIC | 7 | Herbert Küppisch | 19 | | |
| **U-101** | VIIB | 7 | Ernst Mengersen | 19 | | |
| **U-103** | IXB | 2 | Viktor Schütze | 24 | | |
| **U-52** | VIIB | 7 | Otto Salman | 24 | | |
| **U-123** | IXB | 2 | Karl-Heinz Moehle Knight's Cross awarded the 26th, given on his arrival | 28 | | |

*Movements*: eight arrivals, eight departures, number of U-boats present in Lorient at the end of the month: nine (second month running).
*Observations*: For the second month running, only one new U-boat of the 2nd Flotilla put into Lorient; the total number of U-boats operational fell to twenty-two during the month, which represented the lowest number throughout the war. On February 4, there was an accident on U-43 at the quay: the diesel engine rooms were flooded; it took several months to repair the damage. In the Atlantic on February 12, the first combined operation against a convoy in naval history, with a cruiser, U-boats and planes attacking almost simultaneously. Five days after leaving Lorient on February 3 for Freetown in the South Atlantic, U-37 spotted the HG-53 convoy and attacked it on February 9 at 04:30: two ships were sunk. Its precise instructions gave five *Condors* of the *KG 40,* which had flown out of Bordeaux in the morning, the chance to sink five others in the afternoon. U-37 continued to track the convoy and sank another ship on the 10th. It also guided the cruiser *Admiral Hipper*, which had left Brest on February 1, in its direction. The cruiser sank a straggler. On February 20, 1941, about thirty captive balloons were installed in Kernével and Port-Louis to prevent low altitude air attacks.

In the beginning of February, the important repairs being carried out on Prien's U-47 since December were finally finished. The equipment was fixed on February 16 and a test was carried out on the quay; a crack in one of the diesel cylinders delayed departure by two days; another test was carried out on the 18th and another problem was discovered; departure was finally planned for February 20. The day before, Chief Electrician Hollstein came to salute his commander; as he had remained in the arsenal for the duration of the repairs, he had been granted leave. Prien consulted the list of those who would be leaving with him the following day; he now only had five crewmembers who had participated in Scapa Flow! Before leaving, Prien and his officers and two officer-candidates had a last meal at *Chez Mélanie* restaurant in Riec-sur-Belon. On February 20, after breakfast in the 2nd Flotilla officers' mess in the barracks, Prien was ready to climb into the conning tower of his U-47 berthed on *Isère*. His friend Kretschmer was there to shake his hand before his departure. Kretschmer, who was due to leave two days later, asked the man who he affectionately called "*Little Prien*" to find him a convoy as soon as possible. They couldn't have imagined that both of them would be sunk in the next fifteen days. On February 25, U-47

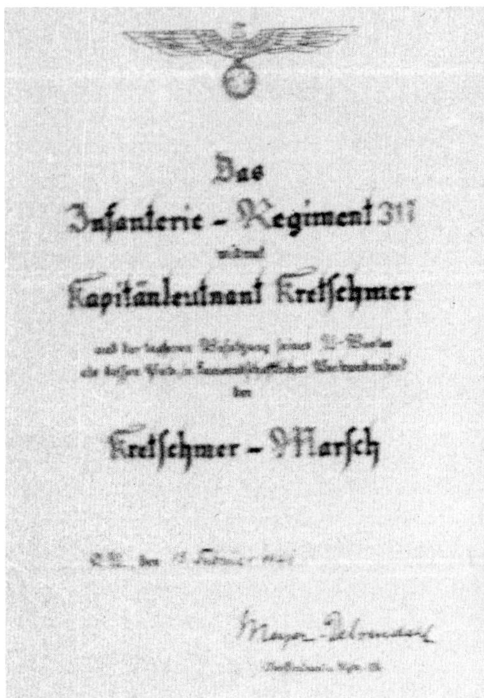


The diploma given to Otto Kretschmer mentions that marching music had been composed in his honor by the regimental band. *LB*

Nicolai Clausen had been the commander of U-37 since October 26, 1940. During his last patrol on December 19, 1940, U-37 sunk the French submarine *Sfax* and the ship *Rhône*. This mistake of sinking two elements of the Vichy Navy wasn't noted in his logbook. Nico Clausen had been Watch Officer aboard U-37 under Commanders Hartmann and Oehrn before becoming the commander of U-142 IID-type U-boat from September to October 1940. *UBA*

Shortly before its departure on February 18, 1941, foodstuff is loaded aboard U-37, in the foreground. Behind it is U-99 that will be leaving for its last patrol on February 22. *UBA*

The insignia of U-106 IXB-type, which arrived for the first time in Lorient on February 10, 1941, was a sawfish painted on each side of the conning tower. During its first patrol, U-106, commanded by Jürgen Oesten, sank the 10,578-ton passenger ship *Zealandic*. *LB*

Filmed by a camera, Commander Otto Kretschmer of U-99 receives a diploma from the Chief of the 317th Army Infantry Regiment, the unit that had "adopted" his U-boat. *LB*

February 14, 1941: U-93 arrives on the Scorff, returning from a month-long operation in the Atlantic, with four pennants. It had sunk three ships from the SC-19 convoy and a straggler from the SC-20, before being damaged by a *Whitley* plane on February 11. It was kept in the Lorient shipyards until May 3 undergoing repairs. In the center: Commander Claus Korth. *UBA*

A buoy from the Greek cargo ship *Aikaterini*, sunk on January 29, has been kept as a trophy. *UBA*

On his arrival Commander Claus Korth of U-93 chats with Otto Ketschmer, who is wearing the Knight's Cross with Oak Leaves. During his classes, Claus Korth had been one of the rare survivors of the school sailing ship *Niobe*, which sank on July 26, 1932. *UBA*

Two officers of U-99, one of which is Navigator Heinrich Petersen who had been decorated with the Knight's Cross on November 5, 1940, are surrounded by the members of the Service of Naval Supplies in Lorient, in a park in the arsenal. *LB*

Commander Nico Clausen of U-37 is welcomed in Lorient by war correspondent Kurt Esmarch. He will be able to tell the journalist that nine days after leaving Lorient on February 3, 1941, his U-boat had participated in the first joint attack in naval history against a convoy using Fw 200 *Condor* aircraft and the heavy cruiser *Admiral Hipper*, which had left Brest on February 1. *LB*

In February 1941, U-65 IXB-type and U-47 VIIB-type are put into dry dock in basin No.2 in the arsenal. The difference between the two U-boats can clearly be seen: much longer for the first and the size of the ballasts on the second. *LB*

On February 19, 1941, U-101 VIIB-type, commanded by Ernst Mengersen, returns from its sixth combat patrol to the west of the British Isles. We can see U-47 alongside the quay; its departure is programmed for the following day. *LB*

After U-101, it's U-94 that returns from a forty-one-day patrol in the same sector. Its insignia, which has been damaged by bad weather and salt water, will have to be repainted during its stay in the shipyards. In his logbook, Commander Kuppisch noted that during the patrol, his U-boat had spent thirty-two days in the combat zone; he mentioned that because of bad weather conditions, it hadn't been possible to use their armament during sixteen of those days, which left justsixteen days of action! *LB*

February 19, 1941: Commander Herbert Kuppisch of U-94 is welcomed on his arrival by Commander Georg Schewe of U-105. This commander will be leaving on patrol three days later. *LB*

The mechanics officer and the Watch Officer of U-94 have respectively received the Iron Cross 1st and 2nd Class, following U-94's second patrol during which three ships had been sunk. They have had their photo taken on the *Place Alsace-Lorraine*, near the *Beauséjour* Hotel. *UBA*

Restaurant staff of "Chez Mélanie" in Riec-sur Belon, Prienand his U-47 officers dined here before going on patrol. In the white blouse is Mélanie rarely photographed without the traditional costume of Aven. *Benoît Senne*

A lot of people have come to say goodbye to Günther Prien on his departure from Lorient on February 20, 1941. *LB*

Günther Prien greets his crew; only five of them were with him during the raid on Scapa Flow; the others have been transferred to other U-boats that needed experienced men. *LB*

The entire crew of U-47 was lost at sea on March 7, 1941. *LB*

The 317th Infantry Regiment's brass band play for Prien's last departure; we can see a back view of him climbing into the conning tower of U-47. *LB*

U-47 prepares to leave the quay for its twelfth and last patrol. *LB*

The departure from Lorient of U-47 on February 20 and U-99 on February 22 marked the end of the period of the first "Aces." *LB*

On February 20, 1941, the balloons against low-level air attack are put in place on the Kernével Peninsula. We can see *Margaret* Villa and a part of *Kerlilon* Villa. *UBA*

On February 22, 1941, just before his departure, Otto Kretschmer has a last drink in the Maritime Prefecture with the officers of the 317th Army Infantry Regiment, the unit that had "adopted" U-99. *LB*

In front of the school for apprentice mechanics, used by the Naval Construction Service, Kretschmer accompanied by the General Commander of the 211. Infanterie Division, inspects an Army company. *LB*

spotted the OB-290 convoy and he sunk two of its ships; he kept it in sight and the next day *Condors* from *I./KG 40* arrived and sank seven more ships and damaged four. This operation was the biggest success for this air group against a convoy. The British nicknamed these planes "the plague of the Atlantic." The U-boat to plane guiding information worked better than the other way round.

The departure of U-99 was also approaching. Back in Lorient from his skiing holiday, Kretschmer went to see Dönitz to ask him if he had given the order to have his memoirs published in Germany. As the admiral was mystified, they searched for the written order. Dönitz had written "*yes*" in the in the editor's letter's margin to say that he supported his commander's wish not to write the book, but his secretary had understood that he meant that he agreed to the publication. Once this was settled, the Admiral sent a letter to the editor to tell him not to publish the book, in accordance with the wishes of the discreet Kretschmer, who didn't want to be put in the limelight more than his combat comrades. Before his departure, a ceremony was organized with the 317th Army Regiment of the 211th Infantry Division based in Lorient and which had "adopted" U-99. In his honor the regiment's brass band had written a song called "*The Kretschmer March*." Kretschmer also had a gift for the regiment: a lifebuoy from the British fuel tanker *Conch* that U-99 had sunk last December 3, which had a message painted on it. As usual, Kretschmer refused to speak into the micros pointed at him by the war correspondents, but it wasn't possible to ban them from the ceremony. A few days before his departure planned on February 22, Dönitz tried once again to persuade his favorite commander

The insignia of U-124 was an Edelweiss, chosen by Commander Schulz in Norway, after being helped by the *chasseurs alpins* in Narvik when his first U-boat, U-64, had been sunk. With U-105 and U-106, these three U-boats were the first of a long series to be sent on patrol in the South Atlantic from February 22-26, 1941. *LB*

The Army's brass band on a ship's serving as a platform, play for U-124's departure. *LB*

On February 23 at 16:00, U-124 leaves for the South Atlantic; U-105 had left the day before. *LB*

On February 24, 1941, U-103 commanded by *Korvettenkapitän* Viktor Schütze, arrives in Lorient after its third combat patrol to the west of the British Isles, during which it had sunk a fuel tanker, two cargo ships, and had damaged a fourth ship. *UBA*

On the *Place d'Armes*, in front of Gabriel Hotel's two pavilions, several crewmembers of U-103 are decorated with the Iron Cross 2nd Class and U-boat War Badge, awarded after three combat patrols aboard a U-boat. *UBA*

Karl-Heinz Moehle received the Knight's Cross from Dönitz in person, on the bridge of U-123. He had been Watch Officer aboard U-32 in 1937 before becoming commander of U-20 until January 1940 and then U-123 on May 30, 1940. *UBA*

On February 27, 1941, U-37 left Lorient for the last time. After a patrol in the North Atlantic, it was turned into a U-boat school in the Baltic. This IXA-type U-boat had, after U-48, the highest score of tonnage destroyed, with fifty-one merchant ships sunk for a total of 190,477 tons, a warship sunk, and a cargo ship damaged. *Anthony Guychard*

The brass band has set up on the *Ailette* platform in front of Péristyle barracks for the ceremony during which the Knight's Cross is awarded to Karl-Heinz Moehle. *UBA*

Recorded by the microphone held by war correspondent Kurt Esmarsch, Dönitz decorates members of U-123's crew. We can see marks on the ship's hull identifying it as the *Ailette* platform. *Charita*

to take a post on land, but his decision to continue the combat at sea was irrevocable. With his new officers and his former Watch Officers Klaus Bargsten and Horst Elfe chosen to follow a commanders training course, Kretschmer had his last evening on land at *Moulin de Rosmadec* in Pont-Aven. U-99 left on February 22 to the sound of the "*Kretschmer March*" being played by the 317th Regiment's brass band.

On February 9, 1941, Churchill gave a speech in which he predicted an increase in the Germans efforts to attack maritime traffic towards England. Therefore he pushed all his forces to make the anti-submarine fight a top priority. As a direct result of this, *Flower* corvettes came out of the shipyards at an increased rate and a QG of the Western Approaches was set up in Liverpool. Its General Staff, headed by Admiral Sir Percy Noble, improved convoy organization and brought new ideas to strategic conceptions. The principal change was in the setting up of escort groups comprising well-equipped, well-trained ships, accustomed to working together to protect the convoys and hunt U-boats.

As results in the North Atlantic fell off between February 22 and 26, the three IXB U-boats, U-105, U-106 and U-124 were sent on operations in the South Atlantic. Between March 3 and 6 they were secretly supplied in Las Palmas, Canary Islands, by the German fuel tanker *Corrientes*; as with all the hostile ships in a neutral port forty-eight hours after the declaration of war, the *Corrientes* had been interned in the Spanish port along with the *Charlotte Schliemann*. Supplied with torpedoes by the merchant raider *Kormoran* and then in fuel by the fuel tanker *Nordmark*, U-105 patrolled in the Freetown sector. U-106 was supplied by the *Nordmark* and in April was sent to Rio to escort the blockade runner *Lech* in the South Atlantic; in May it received supplies from the *Egerland* in order to reach Lorient. After being supplied by the *Kormoran*, U-124 carried out operations in the Freetown sector. The three of them obtained excellent results before returning to Lorient in May and June. However, their days-at-sea results were inferior to those obtained by the U-boats in the North Atlantic during the summer of 1940.

***Allied reactions***: In February 1941, while work on building U-boat shelters was at its height, only one bombing raid with one plane was carried out on Port-Louis and only one mine-laying operation was carried out. Back from operations, the German cruiser *Admiral Hipper* put into Brest on February 14. However, an air reconnaissance carried out over the port in Lorient on February 24 was a herald of an imminent resumption of British raids.

## *March 1941: The Loss of Three U-boat "Aces"*

MARCH 1941

| U-BOOT | TYPE | FLOT. | COMMANDER | ARRIVAL | DEPART | NOTES |
|---|---|---|---|---|---|---|
| Present | | | | | | |
| **U-38** | IXA | 2 | Heinrich Liebe | | 28 | Arrived on January 22, departure after two months maintenance in the shipyard |
| **U-43** | IXA | 2 | Wolfgang Lüth | | | Third month of repairs until 11.05.41 |
| **U-52** | VIIB | 7 | Otto Salman | 23 31 | 22 27 | First departure Second departure |
| **U-65** | IXB | 2 | Hans-Gerrit von Stockhausen | | | In repairs until 12.4.41 |
| **U-93** | VIIC | 7 | Claus Korth | | | First month of repairs since February 14 |
| **U-94** | VIIC | 7 | Herbert Küppisch | | 29 | |
| **U-101** | VIIB | 7 | Ernst Mengersen | 25 | 24 27 | |
| **U-103** | IXB | 2 | Viktor Schütze | | | |
| **U-123** | IXB | 2 | Karl-Heinz Moehle | | | |
| Arrival | | | | | | |
| **U-69** | VIIC | 7 | Jost Metzler | 1 | 18 | First arrival in Lorient, put into service 2.11.40 |
| **U-107** | IXB | 2 | Günter Hessler | 1 | 29 | First arrival in Lorient, put into service 8.10.40; the Admiral's son-in-law left Lorient for his second combat patrol in the South Atlantic, which proved to be the most successful in the entire war with 14 ships sunk totaling 86,699 tons |
| **U-73** | VIIB | 7 | Helmut Rosenbaum | 2 | 25 | First arrival in Lorient, put into service 30.9.40 |
| **U-97** | VIIC | 7 | Udo Heilmann | 7 | 20 | First arrival in Lorient, put into service 28.9.40; Final departure, numerous patrols out of St. Nazaire then the Mediterranean, destroyed 16.6.43 by plane, 26 dead including the Commander Hans-Georg Trox, 21 survivors. Score: 16 ships sunk, 1 damaged |
| **U-108** | IXB | 2 | Klaus Scholtz | 12 | | First arrival in Lorient, put into service 22.10.40 |
| **U-A** | spéc. | 7 | Hans Eckermann | 18 | | First arrival in Lorient, put into service 20.9.39 |
| **U-110** | IXB | 2 | Fritz-Julius Lemp former cdt of U-30 | 29 | | First arrival in Lorient, put into service 21.11.40 |

***Movements***: ten arrivals, ten departures, number of U-boats present in Lorient at the end of the month: nine (third month running).

***Observations***: Arrival of seven new U-boats, above all the U-boats of the 7th Flotilla that were being transferred to St. Nazaire. On orders from Dönitz, who thought that the British had rerouted their convoys further north, U-boats moved south of Iceland. After spotting a convoy and sinking five ships, a pause of several days worried the U-boat Corps Command. There was no more traffic! Then another five U-boats were lost, including those of the three "Aces" Prien, Kretschmer and Schepke, the first three to have been decorated with the Knight's Cross with Oak Leaves. At the end of the month, the absence of traffic south of Iceland and incertitude about the cause of the loss of these five U-boats pushed Dönitz to change the position his remaining U-boats in the North Atlantic to southwest. For the first time since the beginning of the war, U-boats began to patrol west of the twenty-fifth meridian. The results in the North Atlantic fell due to the continual reinforcement of the defense of convoys by more British escort ships. After U-107, which had left on March 29, four other U-boats, U-103, U-38, U-A and U-94 were sent to the South Atlantic to strengthen the first U-boats sent there in February. They had very good results in this sector where seventy-nine isolated ships were sunk between March and July before the British reacted by scattering their ships and strengthening their defenses.

How did it come about that the three "Aces" of the U-boat Corps disappeared almost at the same time? U-47 had left Lorient first on February 20, followed two days later by U-99. When U-100 left Kiel on March 9, Prien and his entire crew on U-47 had already been missing for two days. In the morning of March 7, U-47 had fired its last two torpedoes had damaged two ships in the OB-293 convoy; the two ships were sunk a short time later by U-99. U-47 disappeared in the night of March 7/8, sunk by the British destroyer *HMS Wolverine*, but the British didn't know about this at the time. Given the location by U-110, which had sighted the HX-112 convoy on March 15, several U-boats headed towards it, notably U-99 and U-100. But the message radio was incomplete, it had indicated that only two destroyers escorted the convoy, but in reality, its protection was ensured by the *5th Escort Group* comprising five destroyers and two corvettes! If U-99 managed to sink five ships in the convoy, U-100 was kept at a distance by the escort ships. After sustaining serious damage by depth charges from the destroyer *HMS Walker*, U-100 was forced to surface 1½ hours later. The commander thought they would be safe in the

Kéroman March 9: Fritz Todt, Chief of the public works organization that bears his name, visits the base. He chats with the director of a German firm who has sub-contracted a part of the shipyard. *LB*

commander thought they would be safe in the blackness of the night and hoped to be able to escape discreetly on the surface; but it showed up on the ASV radar on *HMS Vanoc* which caught up with the U-boat and rammed it! Commander Schepke, who was in the conning tower, was killed on impact and only six survivors were pulled out of the water. On a historic level, it was the first time that due to radar a ship sank a U-boat on the surface during the night. Straight afterwards, the submerged U-99 was spotted by the Asdic on *HMS Walker*; well-launched depth charges forced it to surface and it came under gun fire and began to sink. In English, Kretschmer asked the British to save his crew; they were picked up and taken to Liverpool where they began their captivity on land. During his interrogation, Kretschmer was astounded by British knowledge about the German U-boat Corps: they knew how Dönitz's General Staff functioned and the names and the characters of nearly all the commanders, while on the other hand the Germans knew nothing at all about their enemies. The British General Staff used the end of the career of the two "Aces" Kretschmer and Schepke to boost the population's morale. On March 20, Churchill announced the event in the House of Commons and it hit the headlines in all the British newspapers. For the Germans it was a terrible blow; the news about Prien's death was only divulged to the public on May 23, 1941. In his memoirs after the war, Churchill said of the three "Aces": *"On March 8, U-47 commanded by Prien was sunk with its entire crew by the destroyer Wolverine, and nine days later U-99 and U-100 were sunk during a combined attack against a convoy. Each had been commanded by a remarkable officer and the removal of these very valuable men had a determining effect on our struggle. Few of the commanders who followed after them reached their incredible level of capacity and audacity."*

March was marked by several conferences and important visits to Lorient. On March 10, the *Reichminister* Fritz Todt visited Dönitz and saw the office U-boat repairs were planned. Taking into account the increased production of U-boats in the German shipyards, the bases in Brest, Lorient and St. Nazaire would be completely congested by the summer. The outcome of this meeting forecast the construction of concrete shelters for a dozen U-boats in La Pallice and in the two Norwegian bases in Bergen and Trondheim; the protective capacities in Lorient would be increased to thirty units and to twenty in Brest and St. Nazaire. On March 17, a conference in Lorient brought together the German torpedoes specialist, Professor Cornelius and the Chief of the Torpedo Service in the district. It appeared that the torpedoes made in Germany were defective after being subjected to extreme temperatures, as had been the case during the campaign in Norway in April of the previous year. And in particular, the previous month, this torpedo crisis had allowed the OB-289 convoy, attacked three U-boats, to escape with the loss of only three ships; U-552, out of Kiel on February 13 on its first patrol, had fired its first torpedoes, which proved to be defective. U-107 out of Kiel on January 24, 1941, had had four defective torpedoes, five for U-69 out of the same

Kéroman, March 9, 1940: excavating work begins on the slipway, so that it will be possible to hoist a U-boat out of the water to KI and KII. *LB*

Stocks of wood for heating the U-boat base's shipyard. *LB*

Thousands of steel reinforcement bars intended for the shipyard. *LB*

U-107's blazon represents four aces, a reference to Commander Hessler, one of the "Aces." Between March 1 and 18, six U-boats arrived for the first time in Lorient. The first, U-107 an IXB-type, was commanded by Günther Hessler, who had married Admiral Dönitz's daughter in 1937. He had sunk four ships in the North Atlantic during his first patrol. Hessler was one of the rare Navy officers to take command of a U-boat without having been a Watch Officer or having been a commander-in-training. *LB*

Jost Metzler, Commander of U-69, was decorated with the Iron Cross 1st Class on March 2, 1941, the day after his arrival in Lorient. He wore his walking-out dress for the event, which took place on the *Place d'Armes* in the arsenal, next to the bandstand. With his officers, he salutes the crewmembers that were leaving in a truck. Like Prien, Metzler was a former officer in the Merchant Navy where he served for eight years. The pieces of the base of a statue on the right are part of a statue of Dupuy de Lôme (French naval architect). *UBA*

After the decoration ceremony, the crewmembers from U-69 are taken by army truck to the place where they are billeted. *UBA*

Commander Udo Heilmann has a small seahorse attached to his white cap; it is the insignia of U-97 that arrived in Lorient for the first time on March 7, 1941. During its first patrol it sank three ships and damaged a fourth. *UBA*

U-108 arrives in Lorient for the first time on March 12, 1941. Its emblem, a polar bear, is to remind everyone that it started its patrols south of Iceland. *LB*

Commander Klaus Scholtz of U-108 was an officer aboard a torpedo boat before being transferred to the U-boat corps. During his first combat patrol he sank two ships. *Charita*

In March 1941, *Vizeadmiral* Dönitz, with members of his U-boat Corps Operation's General Staff, relaxes on the balcony of *Sévène* Villa in Kernével, requisitioned by the *Kriegsmarine.* On his left is *Korvettenkapitän* Meckel, Chief of Transmissions for the *BdU.* This villa, situated in the Citadel Park, was destroyed after the war. *LB*

March 9, 1941: From left to right: U-110 commanded by Lemp and U-100 commanded by Schepke leave Kiel Port at the same time for the North Atlantic. This was U-110's first patrol and it arrived in Lorient at the end of the month. This was to be U-100's last patrol before it was sunk on March 17. *LB*

The British destroyer *HMS Walker*, part of the HX-122 convoy's escort, sank U-99 on March 17, 1941. As a coincidence, its insignia was a horseshoe, the same as Kretschmer's U-boat! However, the destroyer's horseshoe was open upwards, whereas U-99's was open downward, which was a symbol of bad luck for the British. *IWM*

The British destroyer *HMS Vanoc*, which rammed U-100 when it was spotted during the night of March 17, 1941, thanks to its rather primitive radar *ASV* (Air to Surface Vessel). It was the first time radar helped a ship sink a U-boat on the surface during the night. *IWM*

*Lieutenant-Commander* Donald MacIntyre was captain of both *HMS Walker* and the *5th Escort Group* during the destruction of U-99 and U-100 on March 17, 1941. After the war, he wrote several books that were translated into French and published by Presses de la Cité, under the titles of *La Bataille de L'Atlantique* and *Hallali dans l'Atlantique. IWM*

The British press used the disappearance of the highly decorated Joachim Schepke to raise the public's morale. *Charita*

March 18, 1941: Jost Metzler, commander of U-69, is driven right up to the quay to board his U-boat. *LB*

U-A arrived in Lorient for the first time on March 18, 1941. This U-boat the German's nicknamed *Ostboot* (East-boat), had a mobile gun mounted on the platform in front of the conning tower! Built in Germany before the war with the intention of selling it to Turkey, it became operational on September 20, 1939, just when the Kriegsmarine needed every available U-boat. Its first patrol, in May-June 1940, consisted of transporting bombs and fuel to the Luftwaffe in Trondheim, Norway. *LB*

U-A, whose insignia was a whale, was commanded by Hans Eckermann. Its Watch Officer was Carl Emmermann, on the right in the conning tower. He was the future commander of U-172. The "bathtub" behind is so big that it had two anti-aircraft guns! *LB*

The artillerymen of the *69. Artillerie-Regiment*, that had "adopted" U-69, which had the same number as their regiment, lend a hand loading foodstuff aboard the U-boat on the Scorff. *Benoît Senne*

Jost Metzler boards his U-boat that will be leaving on patrol. We can see several German nurses who have come to watch the U-boat leave. *LB*

U-69 VIIC-type "*Horrido*" leaves for its second patrol south of Iceland. *LB*

left four days later. After verification, the torpedoes stocked in Lorient didn't seem to have any problems. On March 18, a new conference brought together the General Staff of the U-boat Crops, the Chief of Aviation in the Atlantic *Oberstleutnant* Harlinghausen and several Group Leaders of the Luftwaffe, naturally including the *KG 40* 1st Squadron Group based in Bordeaux. Questions about naval/air force cooperation were clarified. On March 23, Dönitz received a Japanese naval commission in Lorient; several U-boats were visited and a conference about their tactical deployment was held.

***Allied reactions***: After a lull during the first two weeks of March, the British resumed their air offensive on the German installations in Lorient, with increased means in relation to their previous patrols. In the night of March 15/16, when the cruiser *Admiral Hipper* had just left Brest for Germany, thirty-six bombers were sent over Lorient but only twenty-eight succeeded in their patrol. On March 20, seven Blenheim bombers out of the eleven planned dropped their cargo on the arsenal. In the night of March 20/21, ten mines were laid and in the same night a massive bombardment was carried out by twenty-one Whitley planes. The biggest bombardment until then took place in the night of March 21/22, when about fifty bombers out of the sixty-six planned bombarded the port and the town. During the same night, between three and seven o'clock in the morning, the German ships *Scharnhorst* and *Gneisenau* arrived in Brest. During the following months, the British concentrated their attacks on this port, leaving Lorient more or less untouched. ■

March 18, 1941: In the South Atlantic U-124 meets up with the heavy cruiser *Admiral Hipper*, which had left Brest three days earlier. *LB*

On the same day the U-boat and heavy cruiser *Admiral Hipper* are together, U-124 receives supplies from the armed merchant ship *Kormoran*. *Charita*

March 21, 1941: the U-boat "Ace" Otto Kretschmer climbs down the ladder from *HMS Walker* to the dock in Liverpool. His status as a prisoner of war begins. During his interrogation, he was surprised by the knowledge about the German U-boat corps that the British had accumulated. *Charita*

March 22, 1941: U-37 approaches Wilhelmshaven Port with a badly damaged conning tower. On March 16, while on the surface, it tried to attack the HX-112 convoy, escorted by the omnipotent *5th Escort Group*, which sank U-99 and U-100 on the following day! U-37 was rammed by *HMS Walker* just as it began to dive and then attacked by depth charges. Once it was repaired, U-37 was sent to Germany where it was turned into a U-boat trainer. *UBA*

In March 1941, three IX-type U-boats are installed in Lorient's basin No.3. On the left is U-38; on the right is U-37. No.3 was the largest basin in the arsenal. *Wolfgang Ockert*

Schepke
Kretschmer
Prien

Was ist aus diesen drei Offizieren geworden, den berühmtesten deutschen U-Bootkommandanten, den einzigen, welchen Hitler das Eichenlaub zum Ritterkreuz verliehen hat?

Schepke ist tot. Das deutsche OKW musste es zugeben. Kretschmer ist kriegsgefangen. Das deutsche OKW musste es zugeben.

UND PRIEN? Wer hat neuerdings etwas von Prien gehört? Was hat das OKW über Prien zu sagen?

WO IST PRIEN?

As the German press never mentions Prien anymore, the British press takes advantage of Dönitz's embarrassment after losing his three "Aces." They drop tracts by planes over Germany announcing the death of Schepke, the capture of Kretschmer, and the uncertain fate of Prien. *DR*

March 29, 1941: Commander Lemp aboard U-110 arrived in Lorient, returning from his first patrol. If the U-boat had damaged two ships with torpedoes, it had also suffered an attack by British destroyers; an accident also occurred on March 23: the gun's tampion hadn't been removed before firing and three crewmembers were wounded. *UBA*

# April 1941: The U.S. Reinforces Cooperation with the British

APRIL 1941

| U-BOOTE | TYPE | FLOT. | COMMANDER | ARRIVAL | DEPART | NOTES |
|---|---|---|---|---|---|---|
| Present | | | | | | |
| **U-A** | spéc. | 2 | Hans Eckermann | 26 | 14 | Transferred the 01.04 from the 7th to the 2nd Flotilla |
| **U-43** | IXA | 2 | Wolfgang Lüth | | | Fourth month in repairs until 11.05.41 |
| **U-52** | VIIB | 7 | Otto Salman | | 3 | Final departure: turned into a school ship, scuttled the 3.5.45. Score: 13 ships sunk, 1 damaged |
| **U-65** | IXB | 2 | Joachim Hoppe | | 12 | New commander, final departure after three months of repairs; sunk par destroyer on April 28, no survivors. Score: 12 ships sunk and 3 damaged |
| **U-93** | VIIC | 7 | Claus Korth | | | second month of repairs since February 14 |
| **U-103** | IXB | 2 | Viktor Schütze | 2 | 1 3 | Departure from Lorient the third on a patrol where 13 ships were sunk, second place in the list of successful patrols |
| **U-108** | IXB | 2 | Klaus Scholtz | | 3 | |
| **U-110** | IXB | 2 | Fritz-Julius Lemp | | 15 | Final departure, May 9, U-110 was attacked by several destroyers and forced to surface; its scuttling charges were defective, the British captured its Enigma equipment; Commander Lemp killed, the U-boat sank on the 10th. Score: 3 ships sunk and 2 damaged |
| **U-123** | IXB | 2 | Karl-Heinz Moehle | | 10 | |
| Arrival | | | | | | |
| **U-38** | IXA | 2 | Heinrich Liebe | 5 | 9 | |
| **U-69** | VIIC | 7 | Jost Metzler | 11 | | |
| **U-98** | VIIC | 7 | Robert Gysae | 14 | | First arrival in Lorient, put into service 12.10.40 |
| **U-94** | VIIC | 7 | Herbert Küppisch | 18 | 29 | Final departure numerous patrols out of St. Nazaire, sunk depth charges from a corvette on August 28, 1942, 26 survivors including Commander Otto Ites. Score: 25 ships sunk and 2 damaged |
| **U-73** | VIIB | 7 | Helmut Rosenbaum | 24 | | |

***Movements***: seven arrivals, ten departures, number of U-boats present in Lorient at the end of the month: six.

***Observations***: Only one new U-boat was affected to Lorient during the month: U-98. On March 22, due to the arrival in Brest of the two battleships *Scharnhorst* and *Gneisenau* needing repairs, 800 German workers were taken out of the arsenals in Lorient and St. Nazaire; this situation caused important delays in the maintenance of the U-boats already in or arriving at Lorient. *Vizeadmiral* Dönitz sent several notes to the commander of the *Kriegsmarine* demanding the return of his work force. Moving U-boat attack zones to the southwest produced better results: the SC-26 convoy was sighted on April 2; attacked by a wolfpack, it lost ten ships. On April 17, as several U-boats in the sector where five U-boats had been lost two months previously didn't find anything in particular, the group moved back to the northeast below Iceland. In Lorient, April was marked by the visit of two personalities: on April 17, *Großadmiral* Raeder inspected the U-boat shelter building site and on April 26, Viktor Lutze, Chief of the General Staff of the *SA*, arrived in Lorient and visited U-94.

The United States, still officially neutral, were taking the British side more and more; in July 1940, they gave them fifty destroyers in exchange for a hundred years of access to the British naval and air bases in Newfoundland and the Antilles. On March 11, 1941, the United States Congress approved the Lend-Lease Program which permitted President Roosevelt to, "*sell, transfer, exchange and lend war material for the good of those countries whose defense is considered vital to that of the United States.*" England was the first and biggest beneficiary. On April 18, 1941, the U.S. extended their neutrality zone at sea, the twenty-sixth meridian longitude west, to 2,300 miles of New York and to 740 miles from Lisbon; in this huge zone covering four -fifths of the ocean in the west, American ships signaled the position of all German and British ships. During the same month, they authorized the access of Royal Navy ships to American shipyards. On June 7, 1941, the United States replaced the British garrison in Iceland and extended their neutrality zone to the twenty-second meridian to include this island; they also escorted convoys from their coasts to Iceland, which was a great help to the Royal Navy.

***Allied reactions***: In April the British only carried out one bombing raid on Lorient; the attack on Brest which had been planned was impossible to carry out because of thick cloud cover. Two mine-laying operations were carried out. ■

In early April 1941, workers of KMW Lorient and crewmembers to fill the tanks of U-52 before leaving on the 3rd. *UBA*

Before departure on April 3, 1941, U-52 commander Otto Salmann is greeted by senior officers from the *DCA* and *Luftwaffe*. *UBA*

April 8, 1941: the foundation of Keroman I has started. In the right background are the Frébault barracks. *LB*

April 8, 1941: the widening skipway requires many wagons to remove earth and rock. *LB*

On April 3, 1941, Otto Salman left Lorient aboard U-52 for its eighth and last combat patrol. Repatriated to Germany, it was turned into a U-boat school. In June, Commander Salman joined Dönitz's staff. *UBA*

In April 1941, in the middle of the South Atlantic, Commander Georg-Wilhelm Schulz of U-124 is decorated at sea by his crew with a homemade Knight's Cross. On April 4, he had received a radio message announcing that he had been awarded the decoration after all his successes. He received the medal when he returned to Lorient a month later! *Charita*

Two crewmembers from U-A take advantage of their leave at the *Grand Hôtel* in Carnac before their departure for the South Atlantic on April 14, 1941. *LB*

Before their departure from Lorient for the last time on April 12, 1941, the men of U-65 salute Joachim Hoppe, their new commander. In exactly sixteen days, without sinking a single ship, they were all lost at sea. Their U-boat was destroyed by depth charges launched from the British destroyer *HMS Douglas. LB*

The crewmembers of U-93 spend part of their leave at the *Grand Hôtel* in Carnac. Following the damage to their U-boat caused by a British plane, they spent nearly three months on land.

Robert Gysae commanded U-98, the only new U-boat to call at Lorient during the month of April. Like Günter Hessler, he came from a torpedo boat and he had won the confidence of the *BdU*, which gave him the command of a U-boat without his having been a Watch Officer nor a commander-in-training. He left Lorient a month later to join his home base in St. Nazaire. He won the Knight's Cross on December 31, 1941. He then took command of U-177 IX D-type U-boat on March 24, 1942, aboard which he operated in the South Atlantic and the Indian Ocean. Gysae received the Oak Leaves on May 31, 1943. He was decorated with the Wound Badge on June 25, 1943, after having spent several hours buried under the rubble of the wrecked huts where the crew of U-177 was lodged, following an Allied air raid. *LB*

On April 15, 1941, U-110 left Lorient for the last time. It was boarded by a team from the Royal Navy on May 9, who captured the U-boat's Engima coding machine. This considerably helped the British Decoding Service's progress. *UBA*

*Oberleutnant* Joachim Hoppe has just been given the command of U-65. Its former commander, Hans-Gerrit von Stockhausen, decorated with the Knight's Cross, has been named chief of the 26th U-boat Training Flotilla in the Baltic Sea. *LB*

On his arrival in Lorient on April 14, 1941, Commander Gysae is greeted by Jost Metzler, commander of U-69, which had arrived three days earlier, and Fritz Lemp, commander of U-110 who would be leaving the next day on his last patrol. Robert Gysae held the fourth place on the list of commanders who had spent the most time at sea aboard a U-boat: 506 days. On January 5, 1944, he was named chief of the 25th Training Flotilla and then, in April 1945, commander of the *Marine-Panzer-Regiment 1*, an anti-tank unit of the Navy! He was greatly liked and admired by his former crew, who told the Americans who had taken them prisoner that he was a great tactician who followed his instincts; he rarely used charts and directed his U-boat by intuition. *UBA*

Heinz Fischer, Chief of the 2nd Flotilla, leaves U-A, whose particular hull shape is clearly seen. *LB*

On April 14, 1941, the U-A left on patrol; it encountered propeller problems and returned to Lorient twelve days later. Commander Hans Eckermann, in the center wearing a garrison cap, was the former Chief of the 1st U-boat Flotilla. *LB*

April 17, 1941: *Großadmiral* Erich Raeder, commander-in-chief of the *Kriegsmarine,* is greeted by Dönitz at Kernevel. *LB*

On April 18, 1941, U-94 returns to Lorient after its patrol in the North Atlantic, where it had sunk two ships and had sent messages to other U-boats that attacked the convoy it had spotted. *UBA*

With its two pennants floating in the breeze, U-94 prepares to berth in front of Péristyle barracks' central building. *UBA*

On April 24, 1941, U-73 arrives on the Scorff, returning from a month-long patrol to the west of Ireland. It shows five pennants, mostly representing ships from the SC-26 convoy, spotted by U-94. This convoy lost a total of eleven ships and a dozen were damaged. Its insignia is the blazon of Duisburg, its patron town. *UBA*

U-94 had two insignia: the ferocious fish biting the British lion's tail, painted on the conning tower, and a metal cormorant attached to the radio antenna! *Charita*

U-94 arrives alongside the quay; four crewmembers are wearing "very British" bowler hats. *Charita.*

The ramparts of Vannes. *UBA*

*Standortkommandantur* of Vannes. *UBA*

After their arrival in Lorient on March 29, these officers from U-94 explore the area: the famous *lavoirs* of Vannes. *UBA*

Commander Helmut Rosenbaum of U-73 is decorated with the Iron Cross 1st Class, the day after his return to Lorient from his second patrol. *LB*

End of April 1941: in hommage of U-47 and Commander Prien, whose death has been officially confirmed, Herbert Sohler, Chief of the 7th Flotilla in St. Nazaire, asked for all U-boats in his flotilla to have Prien's insignia painted on their U-boats. Belonging to the 7th Flotilla, but on call in Lorient at the time and not having a copy of the *Bull of Scapa Flow* to hand, Auffermann, Watch Officer aboard U-69, found several boxes of the French cheese "*vache qui rit*" (laughing cow). He gave a box to a workman in the shipyards as a model for painting the insignia, but the workman simply recopied the picture on the box and added the French inscription, "*vache qui rit.*" *UBA*

The radioman of U-124 before its arrival in Lorient on May 1, 1941. On the left is the famous three-rotor Enigma coding machine. *UBA*

April 26, 1941: Viktor Lutze, head of the *Sturmabteilung* (*SA*) visits the base in Lorient with his General Staff. He is shown how a U-boat works aboard U-94, where we can see Commander Kuppisch on the right in the conning tower. *Vizeadmiral* Dönitz accompanies the visitors with (behind him) the new Port Commander *Kapitän-zur-See* Franz Guilleaume who, at the beginning of April, replaced Badermann, who was promoted to Chief of the General Staff of *KMW Lorient* on April 8. *Charita*

# May 1941: U-boats Are Helpless during the Destruction the Battleship **Bismarck**

MAY 1941

| U-BOOTE | TYPE | FLOT. | COMMANDER | ARRIVAL | DEPART | NOTES |
|---|---|---|---|---|---|---|
| Present | | | | | | |
| **U-A** | spéc. | 2 | Hans Eckermann | | 3 | |
| **U-43** | IXA | 2 | Wolfgang Lüth | | 11 | Departure after five months of repairs, U-43 present in Lorient since December 17, 1940 |
| **U-69** | VIIC | 7 | Jost Metzler | | 5 | |
| **U-73** | VIIB | 7 | Helmut Rosenbaum | | 20 | Final departure, several patrols out of St. Nazaire then sent to the Mediterranean in January 1942 where it sank the aircraft carrier *HMS Eagle*; U-73 sunk by destroyers 16.12.43; 17 dead and 35 prisoners including Commander Horst Deckert. Score: 7 ships sunk, 3 damaged and 1 aircraft-carrier sunk |
| **U-93** | VIIC | 7 | Claus Korth | | 3 | Final departure after nearly three months in repairs, several patrols out of St. Nazaire; U-93 sunk 15.1.42 by depth charges from a destroyer, 6 dead and 40 prisoners including Commander Horst Elfe. Score: 8 ships sunk |
| **U-98** | VIIC | 7 | Robert Gysae | | 5 | Final departure, several patrols out of St. Nazaire; U-98 sunk the 15.11.42 by depth charges from a destroyer, no survivors, 46 dead |
| Arrival | | | | | | |
| **U-124** | IXB | 2 | Georg-Wilhelm Schulz Knight's Cross awarded April 14 given on arrival | 1 | | |
| **U-101** | VIIB | 7 | Ernst Mengersen | 2 | 28 | |
| **U-108** | IXB | 2 | Klaus Scholtz | 2 | 25 | |
| **U-123** | IXB | 2 | Karl-Heinz Moehle | 11 | | Change of commander |
| **U-141** | IID | 3 | Philipp Schüler | 11 | 31 | First arrival in Lorient, put into service 21.8.40 |

| U-BOOTE | TYPE | FLOT. | COMMANDER | ARRIVAL | DEPART | NOTES |
|---|---|---|---|---|---|---|
| **U-201** | VIIC | 1 | Adalbert Schnee | 18 | | First arrival in Lorient, put into service 25.1.41 (first U-boat to arrive in Lorient that had been put into service in 1941) |
| **U-138** | IID | 3 | Franz Gramitzky | 27 | | New commander named in Kiel and change from the 1st to the 3rd U-Flotilla |
| **U-109** | IXB | 2 | Hans-Georg Fischer | 29 | | First arrival in Lorient, put into service 5.12.40 |
| **U-556** | VIIC | 1 | Herbert Wohlfahrt Knight's Cross awarded on arrival | 30 | | First arrival Lorient, put into service 6.2.41 |
| **U-74** | VIIB | 7 | Eitel-Friedrich Kentrat | 30 | | First arrival in Lorient, put into service 31.10.40. The U-74 brought three *Bismarck* survivors back to Lorient |

The two *Dom-Bunkers* built around the slipway in the fishing port in February 1941, are inaugurated in May. While waiting for the other U-boat bases to become operational after the summer of 1941, they allowed two VII-type U-boats to put in dry dock sheltered from bombs. *BA*

***Movements***: ten arrivals, nine departures, number of U-boats present in Lorient at the end of the month: seven.

***Observations***: Arrival of the first U-boats of the 3rd Flotilla while the 7th Flotilla rejoined their new home base in St. Nazaire. Therefore, in spite of the numerous arrivals, the number of U-boats present in Lorient at the end of the month was rather low. The 3rd U-Flotilla *Lohs* had been created in October 1937 with Kiel as its home port; totally reorganized in March 1941 by its new Chief, *Korvettenkapitän* Hans Rösing, after October it would be conjointly based in Kiel and La Pallice. This Flotilla was mainly composed of VIIC-type U-boats. In May nights began to be shorter, which favored the British in its hunt for U-boats and diminished the attacking time for the latter. The group of U-boats south of Iceland was sent west for the first time on May 8, 1941; the OB-318 convoy was attacked and lost nine ships. On May 15, 1941, a second displacement of 240 miles towards the southwest permitted U-boats to find the HX-126 convoy, which also lost nine ships. The tonnage sunk in the Atlantic was also increased by the U-boats in the South Atlantic. On May 15, Italian Admiral Parona visited Kernével. The first two U-boat shelters were inaugurated in May 1941: the *Dom-Bunkers*, which resembled a cathedral's nave to make bombs slide off, were built by the company *Carl Brand* of Düren and started in February on level with the slip-way in the fishing port. With a concrete roof of 1.50 meters thick and an overall length of eighty-one meters, each bunker could shelter a VII-type U-boat. They were used for U-boats until September 1941, when other, more practical shelters were put into service.

In May, the British made considerable progress in the anti-submarine battle. On May 9, a boarding team captured the complete coding equipment on U-110; this gave an incredible boost to Allied deciphering methods against U-boats. Thanks to this unexpected prize, in only a few weeks, the British could already decipher radio messages from German surface ships. Their shipyards produced corvettes and frigates better adapted for the anti-submarine fight and equipped with the most recent tracking equipment. The American Navy, which now escorted convoys to Iceland, freed numerous Royal Navy destroyers for the Iceland-England route; they were able to group up to eight ships per convoy. In May, for the first time two convoys were also accompanied by a catapult ship that could launch a fighter plane; four *Fighter-Catapult Ships* were built in April to fight against German Condors and U-boats; they were soon followed by numerous merchant ships, called *CAM Ships*, equipped with catapults.

On May 18, 1941, the German "*Operation Rheinübung*" (Rhine Exercise) began with the battleship *Bismarck* and the heavy cruiser *Prinz Eugen*. The aim of this operation was to attack Allied shipping in the North Atlantic at that epoch. Notably, it planned to attack a troop convoy heavily protected by seven British warships. The *Bismarck* was to engage the escort made up of the aircraft carrier *Victorious*, the battleship *Repulse* and five destroyers, while the *Prinz Eugen* destroyed the convoy ships. This was what had been planned by the German Direction of Navy Operations. But in fact, the British Admiralty was warned of the departure of the German warship

May 4 at Kéroman: Between the two railroad tracks needed for moving the rubble from the slipway, the first of the "Franki' shafts have been driven into the ground. *LB*

A wooden tower, for guarding the site, has been built on the right of Kéroman I. Below it is the diesel station. *LB*

May 4 at Kéroman: one of the six machines charged with driving in the "Franki" shafts which will give a solid basis to the future concrete esplanade between Kéroman I and II. *LB*

The foundations of the first pens of KI have been laid down, and the coffering of the inside walls is underway. On the left, the wooden partitions of the passages that aren't concreted so that later the workmen can circulate between the pens. *LB*

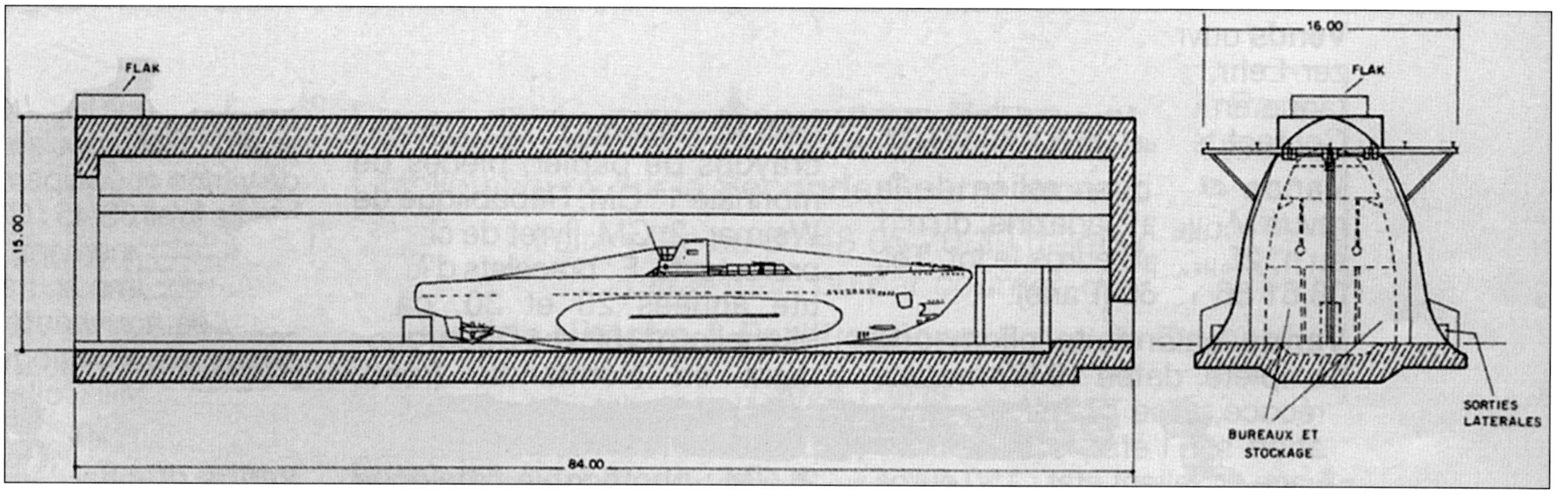


Plan of *Dom-Bunker T6* surmounted by a *Flak* post. *Drawing by Bernard Paich*

May 1, 1941, a welcome set up on a barge to greet U-124. It is the first of the three U-boats sent to the South Atlantic at the end of February to return to Lorient. *LB*

by the British Naval Attaché in Stockholm as soon as it was seen in the night of May 20. Spotted the next day by air reconnaissance out of Bergen in Norway, the battleship was immediately chased by every British ship available from the *Home Fleet* and Force *H* out of Gibraltar. On May 23, in the Denmark Strait between Iceland and Greenland, the *Bismarck* fired its first salvos against the two British heavy cruisers *Suffolk* and Norfolk. Not only did it miss them, but its radar was damaged by the vibrations caused by the guns. The British sent the battleship *Hood*, the new heavy cruiser *Prince of Wales* and several destroyers as reinforcements to intercept the *Bismarck* south of Denmark Strait. A second battle took place in the morning of May 24, when the battleship *Hood* was quickly sunk and the *Prince of Wales* received two shells which forced it out of the fight. However, it had managed to hit the German battleship's fuel tanks, and it lost at least 1,000 tons of fuel. In view of this damage, Admiral Günther Lütjens, commander of the *Bismarck*, was forced to change his plans. He ordered the *Prinz Eugen* to operate alone and continue chasing the British ships on his side. The *Prinz Eugen* managed to escape its pursuers, but it needed to refuel as soon as possible. Brinkmann, its commander, decided to turn southeast to find the supply ships in the Azores sector. The *Bismarck* planned to reach St. Nazaire as soon as possible, but first it had to get rid of its pursuers, the cruisers *Suffolk*, *Norfolk*, the damaged *Prince of Wales* and the destroyers.

When Dönitz heard that the *Bismarck* was in difficulty, he decided to send his U-boats to its rescue. Admiral Lütjens accepted the following plan: several U-boats would be sent to the sector AJ-68, 360 miles south of Greenland, and the *Bismarck* would join them there. The U-boats would then destroy the maximum numbers of the British pursuers to allow the battleship to escape. In the afternoon of May 24, Dönitz sent five U-boats to prepare the trap: U-43, U-46, U-66, U-94 and U-557. U-73 and U-93 would close the trap to the east. Finally, U-111 would join the sector as soon as it received fuel from the *Belchen*, one of the supply ships programmed for the *Bismarck*. Dönitz sent four VII-type U-boats, U-48, U-97, U-98 and U-556 to form a second trap in the Bay of Biscay, 420 miles west of Lorient. U-108 in Lorient and U-552 in St. Nazaire were ready to leave the night of May 25, if necessary. Finally, U-74, even though it had been damaged by depth charges, voluntarily rejoined the second group. In all, fifteen U-boats were used for this operation.

Late in the evening of May 24, the British aircraft carrier *Courageous* joined the pursuit of the *Bismarck*. When it was about 120 miles from the German battleship, it sent nine Swordfish biplanes each armed with a torpedo. The British planes equipped with a prototype *ASV* radar, found the German battleship and attacked. One of the torpedoes found its target. The *Bismarck* wasn't badly damaged by the attack, but the maneuvers it had to carry out caused it to lose more fuel while tons of water penetrated its hull. The battleship slowed again. Its commander decided to abandon the idea of reaching the trap set up by the U-boats northeast of the American coast. He would try to reach a French port as quickly as possible. Dönitz sent seven of the eight U-boats that formed the trap to find the battleship and ordered those in the Bay of Biscay to turn towards the north. On May 25, the *Bismarck*, in spite of its damage, managed to throw off its pursuers. The British, who weren't sure which direction it had taken, deployed the *Home Fleet* towards the north in case the battleship was headed for Germany, while *Force H* out of Gibraltar, comprising the aircraft carrier *Ark Royal*, the battleship *Renown*, and the cruiser *Sheffield*, also turned north. The British code-breakers in Bletchley Park, which could decipher the Enigma messages of the Luftwaffe, picked up a message indicating

U-124 approaches the barge; it has eleven pennants each representing a ship sunk during its sixty-eight-day patrol. The real tonnage sunk by U-124 was 53,297 tons; five ships in two convoys were sunk, mainly in the SL-67 convoy, the six others sailed separately. *LB*

The U-boat commanders and the war correspondents came to congratulate Commander Georg-Wilhelm Schulz, who was awarded the Knight's Cross on April 4. *LB*

The General Staff of the *BdU* have come for the ceremony; from left to right: *Vizeadmiral* Dönitz, his Chief of Operations *Fregattenkapitän* Eberhardt Godt, 1st General Staff Officer *Kapitänleutnant* Victor Oehrn, Commander Wolfgang Lüth of U-43, and Commander Claus Korth of U-93, which will be leaving on operations in four days. *UBA*

Dönitz hangs the Cross of Knight around Commander Schulz's neck. In U-124's logbook, the Admiral signs the following appreciation: *"The attack on the convoy on March 8 proves that the order was a good one* (in one day, U-124 had sunk four ships in the SL-67 convoy) – *in a general way, the very whole operation was carried out with clear thinking and good direction."* Charita

Admiral Dönitz descends to the bridge of U-124; under the directive of several photographers and cameramen, he hands the decoration to Commander Schulz. This handing-over ceremony will be shown in the cinemas throughout Europe that show German current events before the main film. *LB*

Dönitz has just congratulated Werner Henke and Johann Mohr, the 1st and 2nd Watch Officers aboard U-124; Henke will later command U-515 and Mohr U-124. Reinhard Hardegen, future commander of U-123, had also been a Watch Officer aboard U-124 during two patrols from August to November 1940. *Charita*

Dönitz reviews the crew of U-124 that will profit from a long rest. After two and a half months of patrolling, the U-boat will have to remain with the building sites during the next two and a half months. *LB*

Marines of the 2nd Flotilla's ground personnel gather round Commander Schulz to congratulate him. *LB*

Commander Schulz poses on U-124's conning tower, in front of the eleven pennants fixed on the periscope and above the trophies brought back from the patrol: three buoys from the British cargo ships *Tweed*, *Portadoc*, and *Umona* sunk between March 30 and April 8, 1941. As U-124 had helped the survivors of *Tweed* in the lifeboats, the 3rd Officer of this ship searched for Schulz for a long time, and was finally able to thank him during a meeting in England in 1958. *Charita*

Several spectators watch the scene: from left to right: Commander Korth of U-93, Oehrn 1st General Staff Officer of the *BdU*, in the middle in the front: Godt Chief of Operations in the *BdU*, Baehr Flotilla Police Chief and Commander Emmermann of U-A. *LB*

Commander Schulz, whose garrison cap has an Edelweiss insignia, chats with Admiral Dönitz. Like Prien and Metzler, he had spent ten years in the Merchant Navy before the war. *LB*

When he was awarded the Knight's Cross, Schulz entered the closed circle of "Aces." After a last patrol on U-124, he was named Chief of the 6th U-boat Flotilla in St. Nazaire on September 22, 1941.

U-124 on the Scorff with its pennants; now the ceremony is over, maintenance work can begin. *LB*

On May 2, 1941, U-101 returns to Lorient from an unsuccessful operation where few ships were spotted to the south of Iceland. It is escorted to the port by two minesweepers. *Bernd Siepert*

A telephone cable stretches from one of the minesweepers to U-101. The rendezvous of U-boats arriving in Lorient with their escort ships was to the north-west of Groix Island at a point agreed upon in advance called "*Laterne*: LI, LII, LIII." *Bernd Siepert*

U-108 commanded by Klaus Scholtz arrives in Lorient on May 2, 1941. It has recently sunk the 16,444-ton British auxiliary warship *HMS Rajputana* west of Iceland. *LB*

May 5: Commander Jost Metzler of U-69, formerly of the Merchant Navy, is sent on a long patrol off the African coast dropping mines in front of large ports. Food wasn't the only thing to fill the U-boat: sixteen mines were embarked in addition to the torpedoes! Commander Metzler knew the West African coast well having served in *Deutsche Ost Afrika Linie* before the War. Later he recounted his adventures in a book "*die lachende Kuh*" (*The Laughing Cow*) published in 1954. At this stage of the war, this operation was the furthest and most adventurous carried out by a VIIC-type U-boat. *LB*

U-93 left Lorient for the last time on May 3, 1941, for its new base in St. Nazaire. Commander Claus Korth was decorated with the Knight's Cross on May 29. After having obtained a post on land, he survived the war and served in the *Bundesmarine* until 1970. He died in 1988. *LB*

After having left Lorient on April 15, 1941, U-110 commanded by Lemp sank an isolated French ship on April 26 then two British ships from the OB-318 convoy on May 9. Depth charges launched by the British corvette *HMS Aubretia* forced it to surface; the destroyer *HMS Bulldog* sent a specialized team to board the U-boat. *IWM*

Commanded by *Sub-lieutenant* Balme, the British boarding team from *HMS Bulldog* approached U-110 while its crew threw itself into the water and swam towards the corvette *Aubretia* charged with picking them up. Two versions are given for the death of Commander Lemp: the first is that that he swam back towards the U-boat when the scuttling charges to destroy it malfunctioned and he was killed by a British sailor; the second is that he purposely drowned himself when he realized that the British team had boarded his U-boat. *IWM*

that the enemy battleship was heading for the French coast.

British reconnaissance planes, which were sent to the battleship's presumed course for Brest, spotted it on May 26 at 10:30. The *Bismarck* was 690 miles west of Brest. *B-Dienst* had nevertheless picked by the radio message sent by the British reconnaissance plane which had the *Bismarck*. Dönitz, who knew that everything would be decided in the next few hours, sent the group of five U-boats in the Bay of Biscay, U-108 in Lorient and U-73, to the most probable sector where the German battleship might be in the evening of May 26. The sea was rough. Towards 20:00, U-556 crossed the route of the aircraft carrier *Ark Royal* and the battleship *Renown*, but its commander was out of torpedoes. He could only guide the other U-boats towards these targets. Meanwhile, two groups of Swordfish biplanes each equipped with a torpedo took off from the British aircraft carrier *Ark Royal*. The second group made up of fifteen planes attacked the German battleship at 20:47, and two torpedoes found their mark. One of them hit the back of the battleship on the level of the helm and propellers, rendering the ship ungovernable.

The U-73 commanded by Rosenbaum was the first to find the *Bismarck* in the early hours of May 27. He was present during a new attack on the German battleship carried out by five destroyers which launched another two torpedoes. The U-boat couldn't engage the destroyers moved too fast. Due to the rough sea, he lost visual contact with the ships. U-556, which had no torpedoes and was almost out of fuel, arrived in its turn, but once again, the commander couldn't do anything to help the battleship. Other British ships approached the *Bismarck*, notably the battleships *King George V* and *Rodney* and the heavy cruisers *Dorsetshire* and *Norfolk*. Alone, with an unmanageable ship, Admiral Lütjens knew that the hand was lost. The last message he sent from the *Bismarck* was at 07:10 on May 27: "*Send U-boats to save the logbook.*" Dönitz ordered U-556, which was the nearest to the battleship, to carry out this patrol. But Wohlfahrt, its commander, replied that he didn't have enough fuel and would have to return to Lorient. The

On May 7, 1941, Auxiliaries from the Army Transmissions Service, whose R & R center in the west of France is a requisitioned villa in Carnac, salute their flag when it is raised. *LB*

Two Auxiliaries from the Army Transmissions Service on the balcony of their room in Carnac on May 8, 1941. Working mainly in communications, they were regularly asked to welcome the commanders during decoration-awarding ceremonies. *LB*

The British took possession of U-110 that was moored alongside *HMS Bulldog*. Several voyages were necessary to recover all the coding equipment and charts on board, especially the invaluable *Enigma* machine. These discoveries, taken to the British Decoding Service in *Bletchley Park*, meant a gigantic progress in decoding German radio messages. U-110 was finally sunk the following day without its crew or any German service knowing that anything of interest had been recovered beforehand. *IWM*

Philipp Schüler, commander of U-141, had been Watch Officer aboard U-100 from October 1940 to February 1941. U-141 will leave Lorient on May 31 for the Scilly Isles sector, close to the Irish coast. In its logbook, Dönitz's staff noted that this patrol was to prove that a small coastal U-boat could be successful in this zone where the sea lanes were busy. U-141 succeeded in sinking a ship before returning to Lorient. *LB*

The battleship *Bismarck* is the spearhead of *Operation "Rheinübung"* launched on May 18, 1941. Accompanied by the heavy cruiser *Prinz Eugen*, it was sent to hunt down convoys in the North Atlantic. It was sunk on May 27 with approximately 2,200 crewmembers, in spite of the numerous U-boats that went to its aid. *LB*

The insignia of U-141, a IID-type U-boat arriving for the first time in Lorient on May 11, 1941. It returned empty-handed from its first combat patrol during which a *Hudson* plane spotted it on the surface fifty miles from the OB-318 convoy and sent three depth charges in its direction. *LB*

Before becoming the Commander of U-138, Franz Gramitzky had been Watch Officer aboard U-A, U-9, U-17 and U-138. *LB*

On May 25, 1941, at 16:31, U-103 commanded by Viktor Schütze sank the 3,575-ton Egyptian cargo liner *Radames.* Having left Lorient on April 3, this U-boat, along with U-A, U-38 and U-107, part of the second wave of U-boats sent to the South Atlantic from March 29 to April 14. During its patrol, it sank a total of eleven ships; among them, the Italian blockade-runner *Ernani* heading for Bordeaux, was sunk by mistake. *UBA*

U-109 arrived for the first time in Lorient on May 29, 1941. It was commanded by Hans-Georg Fischer, who had been commander-in-training on U-38 in September-October 1940. Only one boat had been sunk during U-109's first patrol, whose crew was almost exclusively made up of young recruits. The U-boat had dived dangerously deep during a depth charge attack and owed its safety to the personal initiative of an experienced petty officer. *UBA*

On May 20, 1941, U-73 of the 7th Flotilla commanded by Helmut Rosenbaum prepares to leave Lorient for the last time on its third patrol in the North Atlantic. Saint-Nazaire became its homeport until it joined the Mediterranean in the night of January 13/14, 1942. It sank the British aircraft carrier *Eagle* on August 11, 1942. During the night of October 9, 1942, it carried out a special patrol: depositing an *Abwehr* agent on the shores of Algeria. U-73 was sunk on December 16, 1943. *UBA*

On May 30, 1941: arrival in Lorient of U-556, returning from a thirty-one-day patrol during which it tried in vain to help the battleship *Bismarck*. *LB*

*Vizeadmiral* Dönitz and Fischer, Chief of the 2nd Flotilla, on the bridge of U-556 greet Commander Herbert Wohlfahrt. Below the U-boat's insignia, the tonnage sunk during this patrol has been recorded. *LB*

U-556, whose conning tower and hull are camouflaged by painted stripes, brings back eight pennants; in reality, only six ships were sunk. *UBA*

On May 31, departure of U-141 IID-type for a patrol west of Ireland. *UBA*

On May 30, 1941, the Knight's Cross is awarded to Herbert Wohlfahrt by Dönitz on the bridge of U-556. It had been awarded to him fifteen days earlier following his report of tonnage sunk which pushed him over the 100,000-ton mark as successively commanding U-14, U-137 and U-556. U-556 and the battleship *Bismarck* had been built by the same shipwrights *Blohm & Voss* in Hamburg; when U-556 was brought into service, Wohlfahrt had wanted a brass band to celebrate the event. He turned to his friend *Fregattenkapitän* Lindemann, Commander of the *Bismarck*, who put his brass band at his disposal. After the ceremony, Wohlfahrt created a joke "adoption certificate" of the battleship and promised that his U-boat would do all that was possible to protect the *Bismarck* from any danger no matter where it might be. *LB*

*Korvettenkapitän* Heinz Fischer, Chief of the 2nd Flotilla, welcomes U-109 on its arrival in Lorient. Its commander, considered as being too inexperienced and lacking in self-confidence by Dönitz's staff, was transferred after his first patrol to the heavy cruiser *Admiral Scheer*. *UBA*

Its commander kept the insignia of his preceding U-boat, U-137 IID-type, with which he had been to Lorient in October 19, 1940. It represents the knight Parsifal; as its commander had just been awarded the Knight's Cross, this decoration was also painted around the neck of the U-boat's insignia! *Charita*

Herbert Wohlfahrt had been a helpless spectator during the *Bismarck's* last moments; his U-boat and the battleship had been particularly close. On May 26, 1941, while he approached the German battleship being pursued by the entire British fleet, he saw the British aircraft carrier *Ark Royal* and the battleship *Reknown* passing right in front of him, but he didn't have any more torpedoes. U-556 even saw the planes that would make the Bismarck ungovernable take off from the aircraft carrier *Ark Royal*! It was sent the following day to try to recover the *Bismarck's* logbook, but in vain. *LB*

On May 30, 1941, U-74 VIIB-type commanded by Eitel-Freidrich Kentrat arrives in Lorient for the first time. Three days earlier, it was with U-556 near the *Bismarck* when it sank. On May 27 at precisely 10:36, U-74's crew heard the sounds of the battleship sinking. At 19:30, U-74 discovered a lifeboat with three sailors from the *Bismarck*; it took them on board and returned them to Lorient. Out of 2,200 crewmembers, the British saved 110 other sailors from the battleship and the German weathership *Sachsenwald* saved two. As for the British destroyer *HMS Cossack,* it recovered the *Bismarck's* mascot floating on a board, the cat Oscar! This black and white cat became the destroyer's mascot, but didn't bring it any better luck than it had to the German battleship. *LB*

On May 30, 1941, *Kapitänleutnant* Herbert Wohlfahrt, Commander of U-556, is greeted by *Konteradmiral* Walter Matthiae the new Chief of the Arsenal. The front wall of the Péristyle barracks, which had been white at the beginning of the month, was covered with dark paint to camouflage it from aerial reconnaissance. *UBA*

The three sailors from the *Bismarck* recovered by U-74 arrived in Lorient on May 30. The following day, Dönitz talked with them for half an hour before they were taken by car to the Parisian office of *Generaladmiral* Alfred Saalwächter, Chief of the German Navy in the West, where they remained for three days. From left to right: Herbert Manthey, Georg Herzog and Otto Höntzsch, who have just received the Iron Cross 2nd Class. They were joined in Paris by the two other survivors picked up by the Germans: Maus and Lorenzen, who had been rescued by the *Sachsenwald.* All five were taken to Berlin by plane and after three weeks of leave, they were transferred to other ships. The war continued. *DR.*

other U-boat nearby, U-74 commanded by Kentrat, although damaged, would have to try to carry out the patrol in its place. When it arrived in sight of the battleship, it was still under fire from the four British ships. The *Bismarck* sank at 10:40 with over 2,200 men on board. The British managed to save 110 German sailors but they stopped rescue operations when another ship signaled the presence of a U-boat. Hundreds of shipwrecked sailors were still in the water. Later in the evening, U-74 picked up three sailors. Dönitz mounted a search operation with six ships that spent four days looking for survivors. Only the weather ship *Sachsenwald* pulled two other sailors out of the water. Admiral Raeder finally stopped the operation on May 31.

Admiral Dönitz declared: "*The destruction of the battleship Bismarck proves that the time when surface ships could operate in the Atlantic is past, now that the enemy has made such progress in the organization of its defense.*" This episode marked a major turning point in the Battle of the Atlantic. The *Kriegsmarine's* surface ships had lost all chance of fighting against the Royal Navy, and they no longer played any real role in future operations. The only means left to the *Kriegsmarine* for efficiently fighting the British were U-boats!

***Allied reactions***: The British carried out two bombing raids on Lorient on May 7 and 16. The first, carried out by six planes, hit the *Todt Organization* camp at Beg er Men in Lanester and killed around eighty workers. ■

## *June 1941: The Destruction of Allied Tankers in the Atlantic*

JUNE 1941

| U-BOOTE | TYPE | FLOT. | COMMANDER | ARRIVAL | DEPART | NOTES |
|---|---|---|---|---|---|---|
| Present | | | | | | |
| **U-74** | VIIB | 7 | Eitel-Friedrich Kentrat | | | |
| **U-109** | IXB | 2 | Heinrich Bleichrodt | | 28 | New commander |
| **U-123** | IXB | 2 | Reinhard Hardegen | 12 | 8 15 | New commander |
| **U-124** | IXB | 2 | Georg-Wilhelm Schulz | | | |
| **U-138** | IID | 3 | Franz Gramitzky | | 12 | Final departure for sixth patrol, sunk by depth charges from 5 destroyers, the entire crew saved and taken prisoner. Score: 6 ships sunk and 1 damaged |
| **U-201** | VIIC | 1 | Adalbert Schnee | | 8 | |
| **U-556** | VIIC | 1 | Herbert Wohlfahrt | | 19 | Final departure for second patrol, sunk by depth charges from corvettes, 5 dead, 40 including the commander taken prisoner. Score: 5 ships sunk and 2 damaged |
| Arrival | | | | | | |
| **U-66** | IXC | 2 | Richard Zapp | 11 | 23 | First arrival in Lorient, put into service 2.1.41 |
| **U-105** | IXB | 2 | Georg Schewe Knight's Cross awarded on May 23 given on arrival | 13 | | Return from a long patrol, third place on the patrols rating with 12 ships sunk |
| **U-106** | IXB | 2 | Jürgen Oesten | 17 | | |
| **U-38** | IXA | 2 | Heinrich Liebe Oak Leaves awarded on June 10 | 24 | | Change of commander |
| **U-141** | IID | 3 | Philipp Schüler | 26 | | |

***Movements***: six arrivals, seven departures, number of U-boats present in Lorient at the end of the month: six.

***Observations***: On June 1, U-boats patrolling in the West Atlantic were sent 250 miles farther south but still had difficulties in locating convoys which seemed to slip between them; even when moving even further south on June 6 and 13! Believing the British could reroute their convoys by detecting echoes from U-boats' radars thanks to their goniometric radio tracking stations, restriction orders were given to the commanders on June 9: only important tactical messages should be sent from ships while in operation zones. On June 20, when Dönitz ordered his U-boats to return north, U-203 sighted two convoys, but because U-boats were widespread, wolfpack attacks were difficult; therefore they were all repatriated to the east at the end of the month. U-203 had also encountered the American battleship *USS Texas* in the blockade zone! For the moment orders were very clear: avoid at all costs torpedoing an American ship, even in a war zone, in order not to provoke the U.S. into entering the war. A single new U-boat, U-66, arrived in Lorient in June 1941.

In May, in order to allow the *Bismarck* and the *Prinz Eugen* to carry out their operation in the Atlantic, the German Direction of Naval Operations had set up a complete resupply organization using auxiliary ships: the two scout ships *Gonzenheim* and *Kota Pinang* put out of La Pallice respectively on May 17 and 18 to reach their position in the North Atlantic; the two fuel supply tankers *Weissenburg* and *Heide* set out to get into position in the freezing Arctic Ocean between May 20 and 22; the fuel tankers *Belchen* and *Lothringen* were sent to the North Atlantic near the North American coast; the fuel tankers *Esso Hamburg*, *Friedrich Breme* and *Spichern* in the mid-Atlantic in the Azores sector and finally the four trawlers *Freese*, *Muenchen*, *August Wriedt*, and *Lauerburg* were in charge of weather reports. Already, in May, the British had captured two weather ships, the *Muenchen* on May 7 and the *August Wriedt* on May 29. Later, after the destruction of the *Bismarck*, which had been given top priority, and the retreat of the *Prinz Eugen* which reached Brest on June 1, thanks to deciphering German surface ships' radio messages, the British began their systematic destruction.

On June 3, the first to be destroyed was the 6,367-ton fuel tanker *Belchen*, attacked by the British cruisers *Aurora* and *Kenya* 100 miles west of Greenland. The *Belchen*, which was in the middle of resupplying U-93 when it was attacked, was scuttled. The U-boat dived and left, it resurfaced

*Oberleutnant* Adalbert "Adi" Schnee arrived in Lorient for the first time as Commander of U-201 on May 18, 1941, and left again on June 8. He had been Otto Kretschmer's Watch Officer on U-23 from September 1937 to January 1940. He had carried out five combat patrols on this U-boat before following a commander-in-training course and taking command of U-60 in 1940. He had been named Commander of U-201 on January 25, 1941. *LB*

June 24, 1941: the walls of the future slipway are concreted; there are still a lot of rocks to be dug out before reaching the desired level. *LB*

later to recover fifty survivors from the *Belchen* who it took back to St. Nazaire. Following the loss of this resupply ship, U-boat operations planned in this sector had to be cancelled. June 4 marked the loss of three other German supply ships: the 4,103-ton cargo ship *Gonzenheim* had received orders to return to the French coast on May 31; on June 4 at 15:56, it signaled that thanks to its speed, it had managed to escape a British auxiliary cruiser but a plane still had it in view. At 20:30, it was approached by the British battleship *Nelson* and cruiser *Neptune*: the only choice was to scuttle it. The fuel tanker *Esso Hamburg* suffered a similar fate: sent on May 28 to resupply U-boats nearly out of fuel, it was spotted on June 4 by the British cruiser *London* and the destroyer *Brilliant*; in accordance with orders, Commander German scuttled his ship. Finally, on the same day, the British had an unexpected catch thanks to the treason of a German captain, commander of the fuel tanker *Gedania*; weighing 8,923 tons and built in 1919 in Kiel, this tanker left St. Nazaire with fuel and torpedoes on May 29; its captain,

Close-up of the metal elements constituting the principal framework of KI's roof. *LB*

At the beginning of June 1941, the back and the interior walls of Kéroman I were built. In the foreground, the space between KI and KII was concreted and rails were installed. This would make it possible for the future mobile platform to take a U-boat to an empty cell. *LB*

June 24, 1941: the first metal elements of KI's roof are put in place. *LB*

The very dense iron framework with spiral steel reinforcement bars inside the roof elements. *LB*

*Oberleutnant* Franz Gramitzky left Lorient for the last time aboard U-138 on June 12, 1941, on a patrol west of Gibraltar. It was spotted there on June 18 by five British destroyers heading for Gibraltar to refuel. The U-boat was sunk by depth charges but the entire crew was picked up unharmed by the destroyers. *LB*

H. Paradeis had done everything he could to delay the departure of his ship. On June 4, the British auxiliary ship *HMS Marsdale* spotted the tanker and was astonished to see it stop without being ordered. The German crew then put the lifeboats in the water before the British even realized that it was a German ship! The British crew inspected the ship and found that it didn't have any destruction charges! They picked up the German sailors and a special team sailed the tanker to England, which it reached on June 12. The German captain hadn't only avoided scuttling his ship; he hadn't destroyed any of the secret documents on board either! The documents seized by the British were very useful. They contained important information about the distribution of Allied forces, U-boats' operation sectors in the North Atlantic, the position of a weather ship, the routes to take when sending captured material, the approaches to the Bay of Biscay and the access channels to the port, as well as the special orders for resupplying the surface ships and U-boats working with them, the orders for meeting with the fuel tanker *Egerland* that the *Gedania* would be replacing, and the exact position of the secret rendezvous points *Green, Red, Black* and *White*! This information of capital importance for the British and it enabled them to continue to destroy the resupply ships one by one. As an extra bonus, the Germans knew nothing of this treason. On June 5, *Egerland*, the ship carrying supplies for U-boats and which had replaced the *Nordmark* in the South Atlantic was sunk by two British cruisers. For the moment, only four German fuel tankers had managed to escape the British trap that was closing around them: the *Weissenburg*, the *Heide*, the *Spichern* and the *Kota Pinang*; the latter two reached St. Nazaire respectively June 7 and 10. The systematic destructions continued: on June 12, the *Friedrich Breme*; on June 15, the *Lothringen* from which Enigma coding equipment was recovered; on June 21, the blockade runner *Babitonga* and on June 23 the supply ship *Alstertor*. The two remaining weather ships were lost during the same period and on the *Lauenburg* the British captured the new Enigma equipment which included the codes for July 1941! The end of June 1941 saw the almost total destruction of the German resupply system in the Atlantic. These irreplaceable losses for the *Kriegsmarine* not only affected the surface ships but also U-boats' current operations, notably those west of the African coast cut off from their supply ships, one by one they were forced to return to their home ports in France.

***Allied reactions***: The British only carried out one mine-laying operation; two of the four planes planned succeeded in their patrol. ■

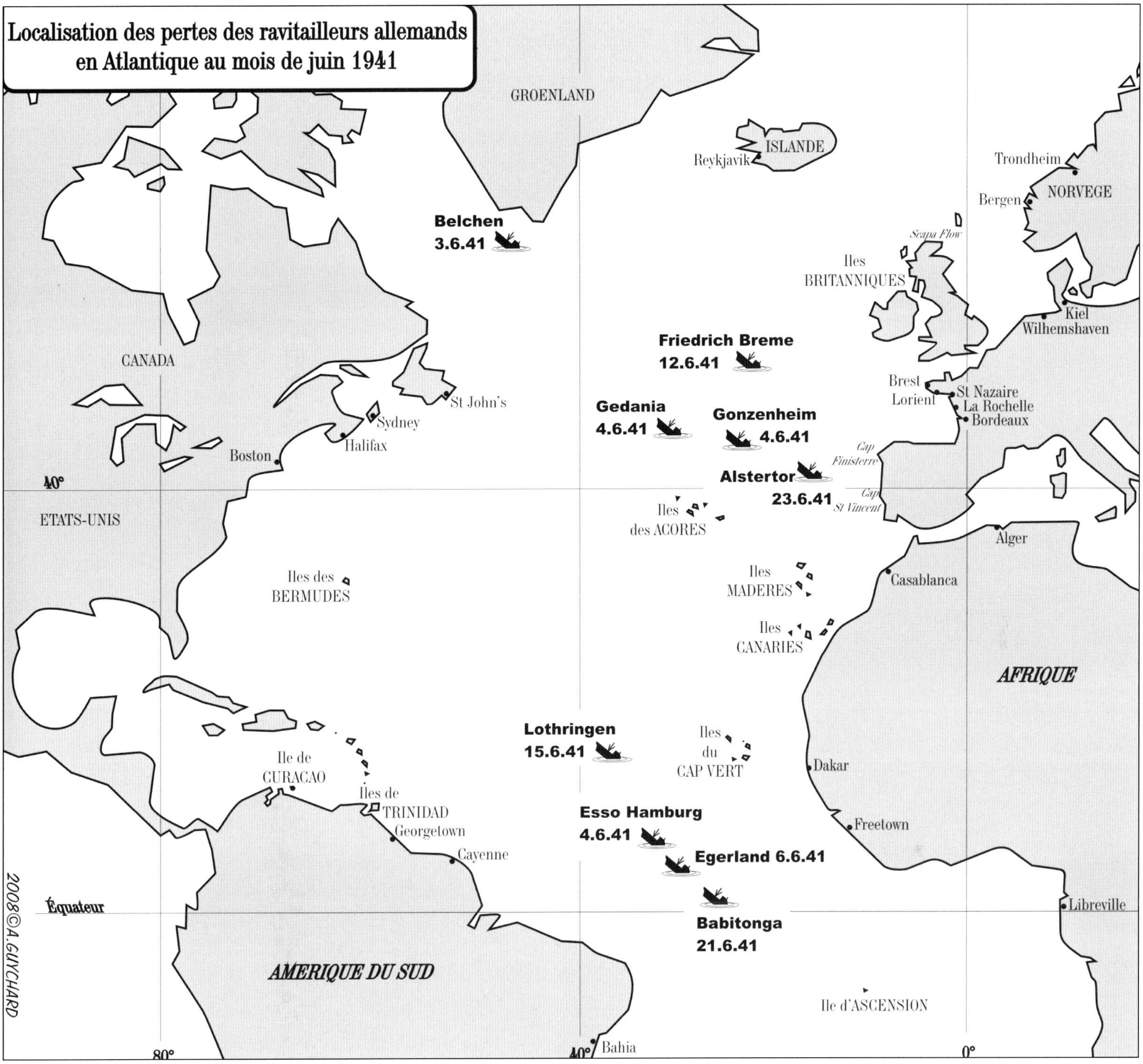

After 112 days at sea, U-105 approaches Lorient on 13 June 1941, returning from a long South Atlantic patrol begun on February 22. *Charita*

Commander Georg Schewe of U-105 brings back thirteen pennants hung on top of the periscope, representing 89,278 tons of ships sunk. *UBA*

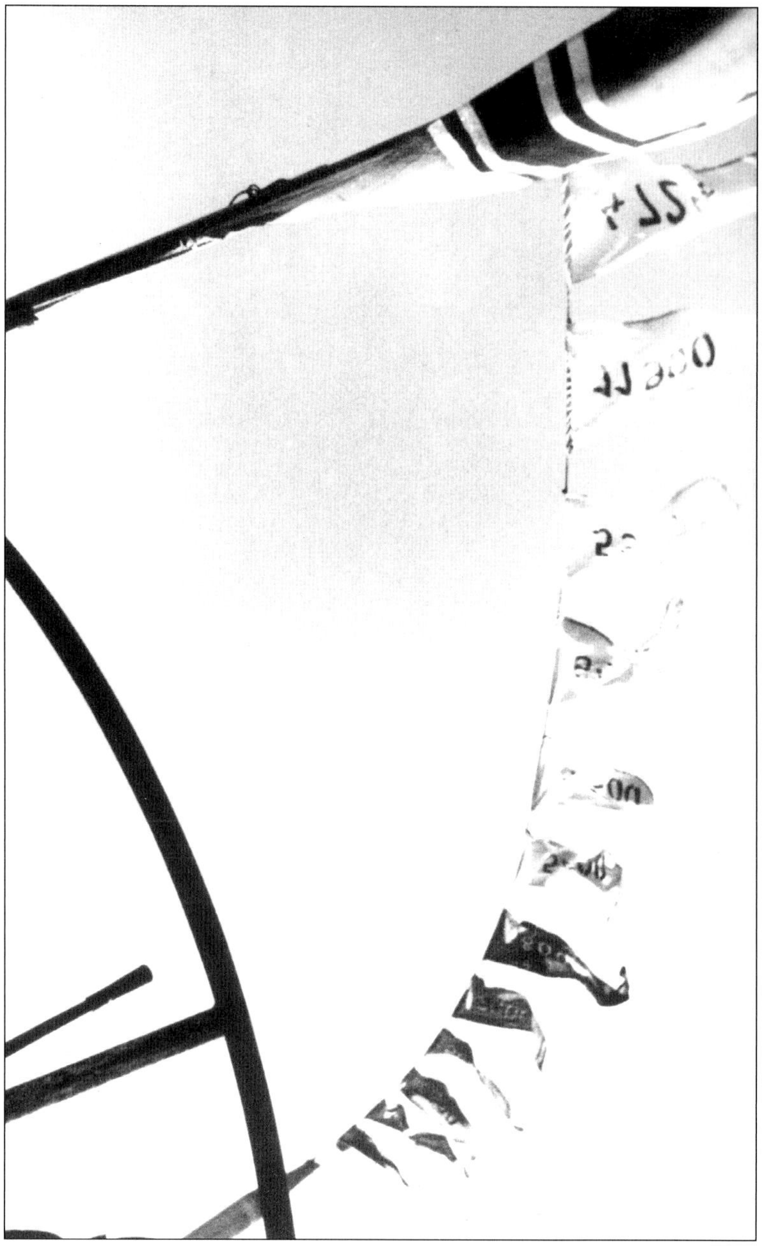

Twelve pennants are shown in this photo, which corresponds to U-105's actual results during this patrol: twelve ships were sunk for a total of 71,450 tons, which represents the second most effective U-boat patrol during the entire War. *Charita*

The decoration-awarding ceremony on the bridge of U-105 is filmed by a war correspondent cameraman. *LB*

On his arrival with the port, Georg Schewe receives the Knight's Cross from Dönitz. He had been awarded the decoration on May 23, 1941, by the High Command and Schewe had learned of it by radio two days later. *Charita*

Dönitz shakes hands with Georg Schewe. In his logbook on this day, the Admiral notes that he had been right to trust this Commander who, up until this last patrol, hadn't had much success. Indeed, on six patrols as Commander of U-60 IIC-type between November 1939 and June 1940, Schewe had only sunk one ship. *Charita*

After 112 days spent on patrol at sea, Schewe is rewarded by a kiss! *Charita*

Commander Schewe on the bridge of the ship being used as a berthing platform for U-105 receiving a bouquet of flowers from the Army Transmissions Auxiliaries *Einsatztrupp 152* based in Vannes. *UBA*

Accompanied by *Konteradmiral* Walter Matthiae, Director of the Shipyard, Schewe salutes the crew of U-105. *UBA*

He inspects the 2nd Flotilla's Honor Company lined up in front of the mechanic's apprentices' barracks. *Charita*

After the ceremony, Schewe chats with an Italian naval officer. *LB*

Georg Schewe carried out two more patrols as commander of U-105 before taking a post on land. In January 1942, he was named 1st Officer of U-boat Command in the Mediterranean's General Staff; in September 1944, he became Chief of the 33rd U-boat Training Flotilla in Flensburg. *LB*

U-106 arrives on the right bank of the Scorff. The tonnage of each ship considered sunk was carefully noted on each pennant; however the pennants with a round number are only estimations. Identifying ships is sometimes difficult, especially at night. Of the ten boats attacked by U-106, five were in convoy and five were sailing alone. In addition to its insignia representing a sawfish painted on each side of the conning tower, U-106 has a battleaxe flag on a mast fixed to the conning tower. Behind Commander Oesten is a cameraman who had filmed the U-boat's arrival at the quay. *Charita*

Commander Jürgen Oesten, who received the Knight's Cross and a bouquet of roses, greets two nurses of the German Red Cross.

On June 17, 1941, preparation for inspecting the troops by Commander Oesten, who has just won the Knight's Cross. The crew is lining up opposite the barracks' central building. *LB*

On June 19, 1941, U-556, commanded by Herbert Wohlfahrt, seen here in the park in front of Kerlilon Villa in Kernével, left Lorient for its second and last patrol. Without sinking any ships during this patrol, the U-boat was sunk on June 27, southwest of Iceland, nine days after its departure. It didn't survive an attack by three British corvettes that depth charged it for seven and a half-hours; when it was forced to surface, the corvettes fired at it and five crewmembers were killed. Commander Wohlfahrt and thirty-seven other submariners were taken prisoner. The commander was a prisoner of war until July 1947. *LB*

Oesten recounts his patrol to his comrades, in particular, Wohlfahrt in the center. In addition to its usual patrols, U-106 went to Rio de Janeiro to escort the German blockade-runner *Lech* across the South Atlantic! *LB*

Commander Oesten, a bunch of flowers in his hand and the Knight's Cross around his neck, inspects the troops. Behind him we can see a chest full of fire-fighting material. *LB*

The Army's band is in place, as well as the 2nd Flotilla's Honor Company aligned in front of the building used by the unit in charge of barrage weapons, the "*Sperrwaffenkommando*"; in the bottom of the photo: workmen from *KMW Lorient*. *LB*

Accompanied by *Konteradmiral* Matthiae, Director of *KMW Lorient*, the commander of U-106 greets the officers of the Flotilla. *LB*

In the foreground: *Kapitän-zur-See* Godt, Chief of the Operations Department of the *BdU*. *LB*

After their arrival, the submariners of U-106 who hadn't gone to Germany on leave were taken by bus to the *Grand Hotel* in Carnac for R & R. *LB*

Several crewmembers posing on the balcony of the *Grand Hotel* with their Chief Engineer, *Oberleutnant* Herbert Panknin. *LB*

These submariners of U-106 smoking cigarettes in front of a villa in Carnac. *LB*

The bus which takes U-106's crewmembers around the neighborhood; the submariner sitting on the right is wearing a miniature metal sawfish on his garrison cap: the insignia of his U-boat. *LB*

A young officer-candidate from U-106 billeted in a requisitioned villa in Carnac. *LB*

These submariners wearing their pea jackets leave for a small café in Carnac. *LB*

Interior of a café in Carnac. *LB*

Photo-souvenir of a menhir in Carnac for these submariners from U-106 in the summer of 1941. *LB*

On June 24, 1941, U-38 arrives in Lorient returning from its ninth combat patrol in the South Atlantic, during which eight ships were sunk for a total of 47,279 tons. However, the U-boat was forced to cut its patrol in the sector short because the British had sunk its surface supply ship. The welcome is very cordial for this commander who won Oak Leaves for his Knight's Cross on June 10. *UBA*

The army band has set up along *Saltzwedel Kaserne*; cameramen prepare to film the troop-inspection ceremony with Commander Liebe. There is no decoration-awarding ceremony, as Oak Leaves were awarded in Germany. *LB*

Dönitz makes a congratulatory speech to the crew of U-38. *LB*

Heinrich Liebe salutes the army band that belongs to 211th Infantry Division. *LB*

To return to the platform, they both go up into the conning tower to borrow an accommodation ladder leaning on the "tub's" railing. We can see the Cupid insignia on the left of U-38's conning tower. *UBA*

The crew of U-38 line up along the quay. Their mismatched uniforms without any panache, which are worn in the confined space of the U-boat, contrast with the usual solemnity of this kind of ceremony. *LB*

Commander Liebe chats with the Army Transmissions Auxiliaries. *UBA*

Commander Liebe after the ceremony, wearing simple work fatigues. He poses in front of the pennants that are still hanging from U-38's periscope. After the War, he returned to his hometown of Thuringe, West Germany, where he lived peacefully until his death in 1997. *LB*

He greets the Auxiliaries one by one. *LB*

Liebe signs autographs for them. At that time, the number of submariners awarded this decoration and still alive to wear it could be counted on the fingers of one hand. They were regarded as real stars in Germany. *LB*

On the Scorff, foodstuffs are embarked onboard U-109 which will be leaving for its second combat patrol on June 28, 1941. *UBA*

Heinrich Liebe in a Navy car. He was given a post on land on July 15, 1941, being appointed to the Direction of Naval Operations within the *Kriegsmarine's* High Command. In September 1944, he reached the rank of *Fregattenkapitän*. *LB*

U-38 stayed for nearly six weeks in the shipyards before setting out again with a new commander. *LB*

# CONCLUSION

By the spring of 1941, the first generation of commanders trained in peacetime that Dönitz nicknamed his "old guard," had either disappeared during operations or had accepted posts on land. They were replaced by a second generation of commanders, also trained in peacetime, who had been Watch Officers on U-boats commanded by the first "Aces." The "*Happy Days*" that the German submariners had lived in during the winter of 1940 out of Lorient, during which targets were numerous and almost defenseless, were over. Convoys bound for the United States were now protected by more and more escort ships throughout their voyage. However, the amount of tonnage sunk remained high thanks to the increased production of new U-boats in Germany: about twenty each month. Taking into account the necessary training period, for the first time, in July the number of operational U-boats was higher than at the beginning of the war. However, after Germany attacked the USSR on June 22, 1941, the Navy Operations Command asked for four to six U-boats to be sent to the Arctic Ocean. Dönitz couldn't oppose this, even if he saw small results compared to his usual operation zones. The more land operations spread, as in North Africa where Rommel arrived in February 1941, the more U-boats were rerouted from their hunting grounds in the North Atlantic. Even if they were more and more numerous, the U-boats were sometimes requisitioned to serve as weather stations for the Luftwaffe or as escorts for blockade runners; not only did their results fall off, but they couldn't carry out reconnaissance for the others, which reduced global results. In addition, in June the British put into service the first aircraft carrier escort ship, a new weapon that would soon prove to be a fearsome obstacle for U-boats. In the near future, American shipyards would produce about fifty aircraft carriers. During the same month, the Royal Navy adopted a new radio message encrypting system that took *B-Dienst* eight months to decipher. After the summer of 1941, deprived of information about convoy routes and supply ships for operating in the South Atlantic, the German U-boats were to regroup in the North Atlantic, west of the British Isles. They would have to try to forge a passage to the convoy cargo ships through Allied escort ships that were increasingly better equipped and better trained. They would have to endure hard times in the coming months. They would have to wait until the beginning of 1942, and the attacks along the American eastern coast, before they could live a new "Golden Age" which would produce a new crop of "Aces."

# GLOSSARY

## Allied terms

**Asdic:** *(Allied Submarine Detection Investigation Committee)*: an apparatus that detected U-boats underwater, called Sonar by the Americans

**ASV:** (Air to Surface Vessel): radar used by the Allies from the air to the surface of the water

**CAM:** *(Catapult-Armed Merchantman)*: Merchant ship equipped with a catapult to launch a plane in case of attack; if it was far from a ground base, the plane was lost and its pilot had to try to get back to his ship

**HMAS:** His Majesty's Australian Ship

**HMCS:** His Majesty's Canadian Ship

**HMS:** His Majesty's Ship

**HMT:** His Majesty's Transport

**RAAF:** Royal Australian Air Force

**RAF:** Royal Air Force

**RCAF:** Royal Canadian Air Force

**RN:** Royal Navy

**USAAF:** United States Army Air Forces

**USCG:** United States Coast Guard

USN: United States Navy

## German terms

**aD** *(ausser Dienst)*: taken out of service

**BdU** *(Befehlshaber der Unterseeboote)*: Commander-in-Chief of the U-boat Corps

**BRT** *(Brutto Register Tonnen)*: Gross register metric tons (of a ship)

**D-Maschine:** Diesel engine

**E-Maschine:** electric engine

**EMA, EMB; EMC** *(Einheitsmine Type A, B, C)*: Mine type A, B, C

**Enigma:** radio message encrypting machine

**Flak** *(Fliegerabwehrkanone)*: anti-aircraft gun

**Funkbeobachtungsdienst ou B-Dienst:** radio observation service for the U-boat Corps Command

**GRT** *(Gross Register Tonnen)*: Gross Register Tonnage

**iD** *(im Dienst)*: in service

**IWO** *(Erste Wach Offizier)*: Watch Officer, 1st Watchcrew Officer

**IIWO:** 2nd Watchcrew Officer

**IIIWO:** 3rd Watchcrew Officer, usually the Navigation Officer

**KMW – Kriegsmarinewerft:** War Navy shipyard

**LI** *(Leitender Ingenieur)*: Chief Engineeer

**ObdM** *(Oberbefehlshaber der Marine)*: Commander-in-chief of the German Navy

**OKM** *(Oberkommando der Marine)*: High Command of the German Navy

**SKL** *(Seekriegsleitung)*: Maritime Warfare Command

**UZO** *(Überwasserzieloptik)*: special binoculars for surface objects linked to a calculator that transmitted target settings for torpedoes

**Wabos** *(Wasser Bomben)*: depth charge

**Wintergarten:** platform immediately aft of the bridge upon which anti-aircraft guns were mounted

# BIBLIOGRAPHY


*Album mémorial La Bretagne en guerre collective,* Heimdal, 1994.

*Album mémorial la Kriegsmarine en France, collective,* Heimdal, 1997.

Arata, Rear-Admiral, *Les villas de Kernevel,* Marine Nationale, 1990.

Blair, Clay, *Hitler's U-Boat War, two volumes,* Cassell & Co., 2000.

Bohn, Roland, *Raids aériens sur la Bretagne durant la second guerre mondiale,* vols. 1 and 2, Vanity Press, 1997-1998.

Bourguet-Maurice, Louis and Grand Colas, Josyane, *Et la tannière devint le village,* Du Quantième, 1997.

Braeuer, Luc, *La base de submarines de Lorient,* 2008.

Busch, Rainer and Roll, Hans-Joachim, *Der U-boat Krieg,* vols. 1-5, Mittler Verlag, 1996-2003.

Caroff, Commander, *Les Forces Maritimes de l'Ouest 1939-1940,* General Staff, General of the Marine Nationale, 1954.

Chazette, Alain, articles in *39/45 Magazines,* n°241 and 243, 2007.

Dönitz, Karl, *Ten Years and Twenty Days,* Plon, 1959.

Dörr, Manfred, *Die Ritterkreuzträger der U-Boot-Waffe,* Biblio Verlag, 1988.

Fahrmbacher, Wilhelm and Matthiae, Walter, *Lorient,* Prinz Eugen Verlag, 1956.

Frank, Wolfgang, ed., *U-boats contre les marines allies,* Arthaud, 1956.

Gröner, Erich, *Die deutschen Kriegsschiffe Band 4,* Bernard & Graefe Verlag, 1986.

Hague, Arnold, *The Allied Convoy System,* Vanwell Published Limited, 2000.

Herlin, Hans, *Les damnés de l'Atlantique,* France-Empire, 1960.

Högel, Georg, *Embleme Wappen Mailings,* Koehler Verlag, 1996.

Le Berd, Jean, *Lorient sous l'occupation,* Ouest-France, 1986.

Le Guen, A., *Lorient ville martyre,* Vanity Press, 1991.

Leroux, Roger, *Le Morbihan en guerre,* Imprimerie de la Manutention, 1991.

Lukas, Yann, *Hennebont,* Palantines, 2006.

Malbosc, Guy, *La Bataille de l'Atlantique,* Economica, *1995.*

Mallmann-Showell, Jak, *Deutsche U-Boot-Stützpunkte und Bunkeranlagen,* Motorbuch Verlag, 2002.

Mallmann-Showell, Jak, *U-Boats at War, Landings on Hostile Shores,* Ian Allan Publishing, 2000.

Neitzel, Sönke, *Die deutschen Ubootbunker,* Bernard & Graefe Verlag, 1991.

Pfefferle, Ernst, *Kameraden zur See, Band 4,* 1986.

Puth, L. Le, *Quelques souvenirs de la vie Lorientaise de 1940 à 1945,* 1955.

Rahn, Werner, *Kriegstagebuch der Seekriegsleitung 1939-1945,* Mittler & Sohn Verlag.

*Rapports d'activité du XXVe Corps d'Armée allemand en occupation en Bretagne,* translated by Commandant Even, Ministère de la Défense, SHAT, 1978.

Réberac, Fabien, "La Kampfgeschwader 40," in *Histoire de guerre,* N°12, 2001.

Robertson, Terence, *The Golden Horseshoe,* Evans Brothers Limited, 1955.

Roskill, S.W., *Captain, La flotte britannique en guerre,* Presses de la Cité, 1961.

Schmeelke, Karl Heinz and Schmeelke, Michael, *German U-Boat Bunkers,* Schiffer, 1999.

*The U-Boat War in the Atlantic,* HMSO Publications Centre, 1989.

White, John, *U-Boat Tankers,* Airlife Publishing, 1998.

Wynn, Kenneth, *U-Boat Operations of the Second World War,* Chatham Publishing, 1997.

# ADMIRAL DÖNITZ'S QG IN KERNEVEL

September 1940: the German U-boat Corps' QG settles into a beautiful building requisitioned at 18 Boulevard Suchet in the 16th district of Paris. We can see *Konteradmiral* Karl Dönitz at the center window, on the first floor. This building is located just opposite the *Bois de Boulogne* where Dönitz liked to walk. *Bernd Siepert*

Match-up in 2008. Today the building is an annex of the Russian Embassy. *LB*

Kerlilon Villa, on Kernevel Point on Larmor-Plage, was requisitioned in the summer of 1940 to house Admiral Dönitz's staff. It officially moved in on November 11, 1940. This is a view of the back taken on Heritage Day. The central part corresponds to the large interior staircase; above the window we can see a medallion on which is engraved the name of the villa and the date of its construction: 1899. *Anthony Guychard*

On April 17, 1941, *Großadmiral* Erich Raeder, who is getting out of his car, is welcomed by Dönitz in front of the steps of Kerlilon Villa. On the left is Margaret Villa that had also been requisitioned by the *Kriegsmarine*. *UBA*

High on the left on Kerlilon Villa's front is a medallion bearing the stylized initial of its former owners: the Ouizille family. The terrace we can see is the roof of Bunker No.5 which houses the transmitters used to communicate with U-boats at sea. *LB*

A large spiral staircase leads to the first floor of Kerlilon Villa. The villa, which was bought from the Ouizille family by the French Navy in 1956, is now the residence of the Maritime Prefect of the Lorient district. *LB*

The Transmissions Bunker No.5 located under Kerlilon Villa's front terrace, was entirely paneled. *LB*

The large living room was used as Admiral Dönitz's operations center; it was in this room that the majority of the photos of the epoch were taken, showing commanders studying charts on a table. *LB*

A small bar is immediately on the right when entering. It was decorated with tampions offered by Allied ships passing through Lorient after the end of the War. *LB*

More booty: a wooden table whose top is composed of fifteen earthenware tiles made in Quimper repeating the insignia of the 2nd U-boat Flotilla eight times and seven insignia from different U-Boats. *LB*

Detail of the tiles composing the table-top: insignia of the 2nd U-Flotilla; a frisky puppy for U-507; a Viking ship and a key for U-163; a clover-leaf for U-68, a castle for U-156; a ram for U-67; a polar bear for U-108; a swimming cow for U-154. *LB*

This decorative clock of the German Navy is part of the spoils of war taken by the French Navy after the Liberation. *LB*

View from Kerlilon Villa's roof of the entry to Lorient Harbor; on the left is Port-Louis Citadel built by the Spaniards in 1590. *LB*

Exterior reinforced door leading to the two bunkers located in front of and beside Kerlilon Villa. *LB*

Dönitz's flag can be seen in the U-boat Archive in Cuxhaven. *LB*

Uniform of *Großadmiral* Dönitz on view in the seminar room at the U-boat Archive in Cuxhaven. *LB*

# THREE BUNKERS FOR THE U-BOAT CORPS' STAFF AROUND KERLILON VILLA

Double doors of the passage between the two bunkers that were used by transmissions to the U-boat Corps HQ. *LB*

The large room in Bunker No.4 "Command Center" where a globe and a maritime zone grid were housed. Dönitz's staff could carry out their calculations here sheltered from air raids. *LB*

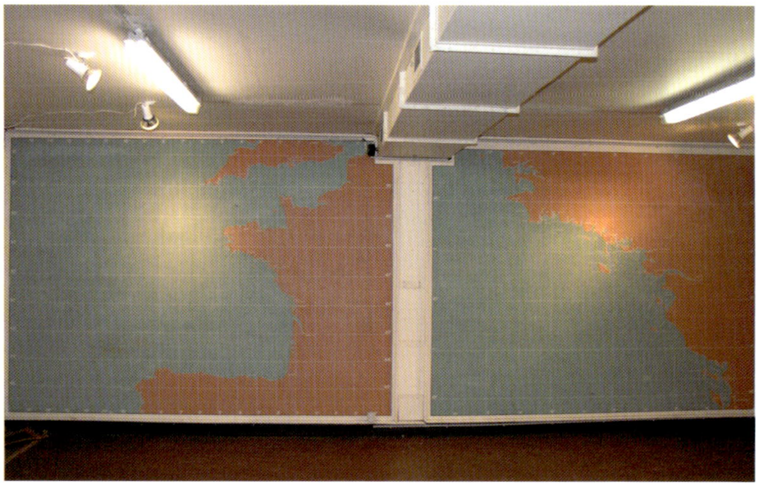

French sea charts decorated the walls of Bunker No.4. *LB*

The interior partitions separating the barrack rooms in Bunker No.1 have disappeared; nevertheless a part of the sanitary facilities remains: a shower. *LB*

An entirely tiled bathtub in Bunker No.1. Over it we can see an air distribution valve. *LB*

The large Bunker No.1 was built at the bottom of Kerlilon Villa. *LB*

Entry to the large Bunker No.1 that was used as shelter for the personnel of the general staff in the event of air raids. *LB*

An *Oberleutnant* of Dönitz's staff leaves Bunker No.1. *BA*

## THE VILLAS MARGARET AND KEROZEN IN KERNEVEL AND BRANDÉRION CHATEAU

From left to right: the three villas Kerozen, Kerlilon and Margaret requisitioned by the U-boat Corps Command. The first was built in 1850 by the Gillet family, the founder of a sardine preserve factory in 1834. When he died in 1858, Kerosen Villa was bought by Auguste Ouizille. On the large grounds of this property, his family built Margaret Villa in 1896 and Kerlilon Villa in 1899. Being used as holiday homes, these three villas formed a single property with only one access road until their requisition in 1940. *LB*

Kerozen Villa was built in 1850 on the site of the stores that were once a part of the Henri Dupuy de Lôme Shipyard. *LB*

Only Margaret Villa hasn't been bought by the French Navy that rented it in 1945; its owners recovered it in 1956. A café has been opened there. *LB*

Brandérion Chateau was requisitioned in February 1941 by the German Luftwaffe to lodge the staff of the Luftwaffe Atlantic Command. *LB*

View of the epoch, taken from the window in Margaret Villa's living room, of the Lorient harbour where we can see a tuna boat. St. Michel Island can be seen on the left. *UBA*

The living room in Margaret Villa with a splendid chimney decorated with the Brittany ermines. *LB*

A sign outside Kerozen Villa announces that it belongs to the French Navy. *LB*

Several buildings were built in the Brandérion Chateau's park for the personnel of *Fliegerführer Atlantik.* A concreted patio with columns leads to a large building. *LB*

## KERLOIS CHATEAU – *WILHELM BAUER KASERNE* IN HENNEBONT

Admiral Dönitz's car leaves Kerlois Chateau that has been re-named "*Wilhelm Bauer Kaserne*," after the German engineer (1822-1875) who invented several models of hand-operated submarines. *ECPAD*

The entry of Kerlois Chateau, which today is St. Felix College (private). *LB*

Admiral Dönitz visits the barracks with his staff. *ECPAD*

The grounds have been concreted but the building hasn't changed. *LB*

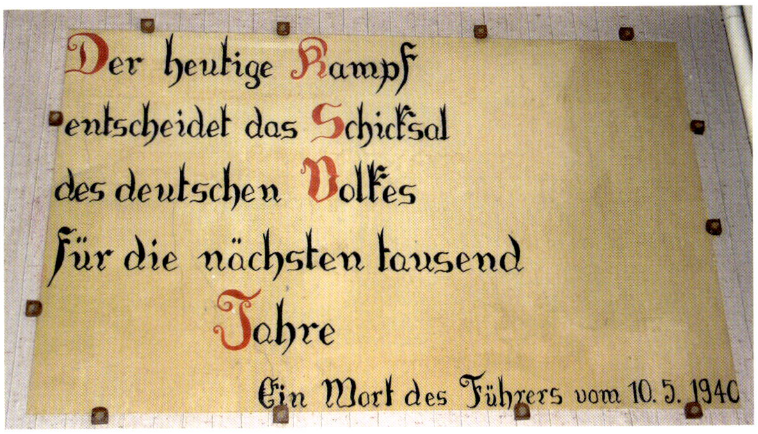


A maxim painted on the Chateau's first floor: "*The combat of today decides the destiny of the German race for next thousand years.*" *LB*

Another painted maxim: "*A day will come where one will be able to measure the scale of all that Germany has achieved with its leader and its soldiers since September 1, 1939.*" *LB*

On a door leading to the Chateau's basement, a painted sign indicating the way to the showers is still in place. *LB*

A room has kept its original door and its painted walls resembling wallpaper. *LB*

## KÉROMAN SCHOOL – *U-BOOT-HEIM*

Kéroman School was requisitioned and turned into a submariners' hostel. Brand new, it had never opened its doors to pupils! *LB*

The elementary school in Kéroman today. Allied bombardments destroyed the other wing but not the principal entry. *LB*

The large reception room on the ground floor. It regularly housed crews returning from patrols. *LB*

The rotunda had been turned into a restaurant. This section was destroyed by bombs. *LB*

Today, this great room is a gym. *LB*

The school's inner play yard. *LB*

Embroidered handkerchief souvenirs, mounted on postcards, sold to German soldiers in Lorient. They had been stuck in one of the three photo albums discovered by the author in 2005. *LB*

There were several large personnel bunkers around the hostel, but today only one remains. *LB*

# THE PÉRISTYLE BARRACKS – *SALTZWEDEL KASERNE*

Three personal decorations belonging to the submariner of 1914/18 Reinhold Saltzwedel are exposed today to the Atlantic Wall Museum in Raversjide, West Flanders. In 1941, five years after the 2nd U-boat Flotilla, this coastal battery was baptized with the same name of "Saltzwedel." *LB*

The two Gabriel Hotel pavilions, seat of the Maritime Prefecture, had been requisitioned to install the German Port Command. In the background, is the *tour de la Découverte*. *LB*

A street in the Lorient arsenal in 1941. *ECPAD*

The same street today, only the building at the bottom survived the bombardments. *LB*

The German Navy also built wooden huts in the arsenal. *ECPAD*

The building has changed since the war but the sub-foundations are the same. *LB*

Platforms are still in place for boats to moor on the right bank of the Scorff, alongside Péristyle barracks. *LB*

The Péristyle quay where the welcome ceremonies were held when U-boats returned from patrols; on the left we can see the personnel bunkers that had been built in the barracks' courtyard and the *tour de la Découverte*. *LB*

## THE BUNKERS FOR THE PERSONNEL AT *SALTZWEDEL KASERNE*

A petty officer gathers a section of the 2nd Flotilla's ground personnel in front of the two bunkers built in the courtyard of Péristyle barracks. Each wing had been baptized of a name of submariner missing at sea since September 1939; on the bottom of one sign we can see *"Haus Kleinschmidt"* in remembrance of the commander of U-111, disappeared on October 4, 1941. *ECPAD*

In 2009, only the two large, two-story bunkers remained and these were destroyed in 2013. *LB*

The concrete staircase joining the first and the second floors of the bunkers, we can see a wooden rifle-rack for eleven *Mauser* rifles. *LB*

Tiled shower in the bunker with a pressure relief valve at the bottom, and an air distribution valve on the top. *LB*

This room contains six electric fans model *HES 2, 4*; each one could bring 2,400 liters of air purified by the filters inside the bunker. *LB*

A "*Sanozon*" air purifier still in place in the toilets of one of the two bunkers after sixty-five years! *LB*

The large rest rooms in the bunkers had been fitted out with vertical bars in the middle of the room and along the walls for setting up the bunks. *LB*

The third bunker for the personnel had been built before sail-loft and the *Cours aux Ancres*, the buildings were destroyed by bombs. *LB*

# THE SEASIDE RESORT OF CARNAC – USED BY SUBMARINERS FOR R & R

The *Grand Hotel* in Carnac, located directly opposite the beach, was requisitioned in the summer of 1940 for submariners on leave. *LB*

The building hasn't changed but now it is a gym for the hotel's clients. *LB*

On the right of the *Grand Hotel* was *Armor Bar* in front of which in April 1941 two crewmembers of U-103 pose for a photo. The second on the right is 1st Watch Officer *Oberleutnant* Harald Gelhaus, surrounded by officers of the 211th Infantry Division. *UBA*

The hotel has now been turned into a holiday home. *LB*

The Miraflore villa, located outside the seaside resort of Carnac, was also requisitioned by the German Navy. *BA*

The same villa today, private property! *LB*

A group of Army Transmissions Auxiliaries come to spend a few days of leave in May 1941 discover the rows of menhirs in Kermario. *LB*

The rows of menhirs in Kermario were set up with the Neolithic era between the fifth and second centuries BCE. According to a study undertaken by three French researchers published in the magazine *Research*, German archaeologists were sent to Carnac during autumn 1940 to carry out land surveys. They wanted to prove that the people who settled in this sector came by sea from the North. *LB*

# THE SEASIDE RESORT OF QUIBERON – USED BY SUBMARINERS FOR R & R

The Commander of U-61, Wolfgang Stiebler, took this photo during the second half of September 1940, while his U-boat was in maintenance in the shipyards. It is Turpault Castle, named after its builder in 1904, located on Beg-er-Lan Point, southwest of Quiberon. Commander Stiebler's original album is preserved in the U-boat Archive in Cuxhaven. *UBA*

This photo of Turpault Castle in the distance was taken on the other side of Quiberon Bay, near the casino. In the foreground we can see the vestiges of a "Tobruk" (shelter named after the Siege of Tobruk) for machine-guns along the Atlantic Wall. *LB*

During the second half of September 1940, crewmembers from U-61 settle into *St. Cornély* Hotel, which had been requisitioned by the German Navy. *UBA*

The hotel located on the embankment of Quiberon was transformed into an R & R residence. *LB*

During the second half of September 1940, the crewmembers of U-28 sun bathe on the parapet of the bar located on the first floor of *St. Cornély* Hotel. *UBA*

The blind with publicity for Lorraine beer *"La Meuse"* has been removed and the hotel has been renamed "*St. Michel Villa.*" *LB*

A member of the crew from U-29 took this photo of Quiberon Bay in October 1940; we can see school children on the left and on the wall on the right the famous German poster printed at the beginning of the War: "*Abandoned population, have confidence in German soldiers.*" *UBA*

Quiberon Bay today. *LB*

Painting by German artist Ernst Vollbehr dated April 2, 1941, representing the formwork of one of the two *Dom-bunkers*. In the foreground we can clearly see the entry of the slipway in the fishing port. *Anthony Guychard*

In the spring of 1941, a U-boat, whose stern is visible, is slid towards the interior of *T6 Dom-bunker* whose entry is summarily camouflaged by two large tarpaulins. DR.

View inside T6 from the back; we can see the offices and workshops on each side of the two floors. *LB*

View inside *T6 Dom-bunker* from the front with its two cranes set up on rolling platforms for shifting material. *LB*

*T6 Dom-bunker* seen in profile. It was 81m long and was protected by 1.50m-thick reinforced concrete in the shape of a nave to make bombs slide off it. *LB*

The slipway's pivoting system that was in front of both *Dom-bunkers* was completely filled in. On the left, T5 used as a four-story storage space at that time and on the right, T6. *LB*

View of the entry to *T6 Dom-bunker* as it is today. The anti-aircraft post above the entry was very severely damaged during bombardments on January 29, 1943. *LB*

View of both *Dom-bunkers* taken from the mouth of the fishing port in 2008. They were no longer used to shelter U-boats after the American bombardment on November 18, 1942. *LB*

## INTERIOR OF *T5 DOM-BUNKER*

A large staircase built at the time in the middle of *T5 Dom-bunker* gives access to the four storeys used for stocking the submariners' personal effects. The photo was taken inside the storerooms on the first floor. *LB*

Each storeroom was closed by two partitions on the sides with grating on the front. The fitted grating on the door had a lock. A small black sign indicated the room number that was given to the submariners. *LB*

On the back of each sign, after the "U," was the number of U-boot, written in chalk and only seen by the submariners themselves. *LB*

A submariner had written "U-123" in three colors on a concrete pillar in the center of the storeroom. *LB*

A key with a metal tag indicating a chest number was found in a room in 2008. *LB*

Example of both sides of the sign. It should be noted that the stamp in blue ink of a 1st Watch Officer "*Lt.z.See U. I.W.O.*" was applied several times in the white space in the letter U. *Benoit Senne*

A room on the first floor without a sign indicating the number of a U-boat but large sign with "PK" on it. These initials repeated in chalk over the door "*Propaganda Kompanie*" indicated that the affairs of war correspondents leaving for operation at sea were stored there. *LB*

Storerooms were separated by grating or bricks. We can clearly see the nave-shaped roof inside the *Dom-bunker*. *LB*

## EARTHENWARE TILES WITH THE INSIGNIA OF LORIENT U-BOATS

The insignia of U-43 represented the seniority rank that German marines wore on the sleeve of their uniforms; it had been adopted as the insignia for U-43 because it was the oldest U-boat in the *Flotilla Hundius*. *LB*

The insignia of U-67 under the command of Günther Müller-Stockheim. *LB*

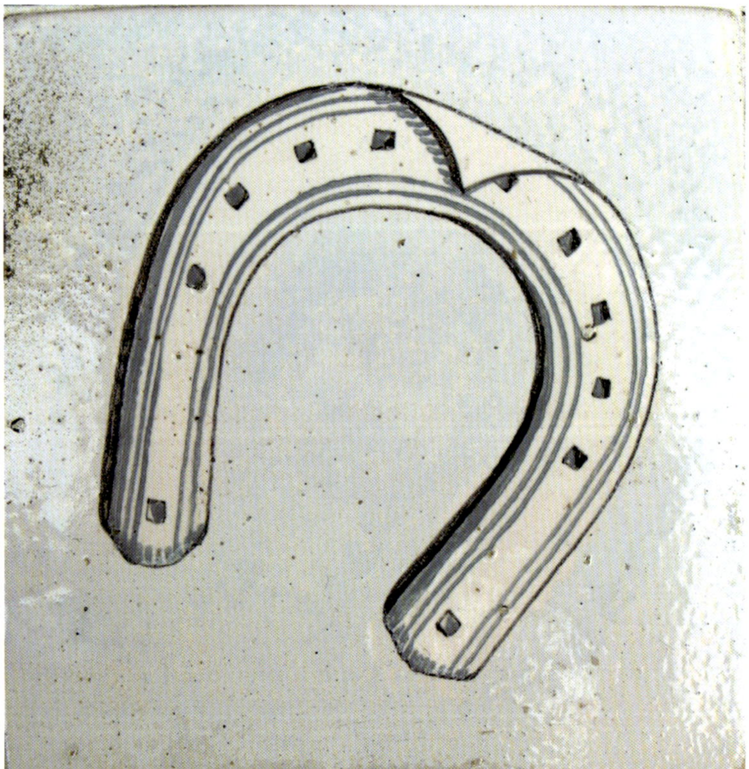

The insignia of U-99 under Otto Kretschmer, a horseshoe opening downwards. This U-boat was sunk by a British destroyer whose insignia was a horseshoe opening upwards, the reverse being a bad-luck sign for the British! *LB*

The insignia of U-105 commanded by Georg Schewe was a blue star that his men called the "Star of Rio," after a famous German film of the same name that premiered in December 1940. *LB*

The insignia of U-66 was a lion's head, the emblem of the Bavaria Army Corps after the First World War. *LB*

The insignia of U-68 under the command of Jost Metzler consisted of a cloverleaf over a chevron. As a sign of seniority, the chevron was awarded after a year of campaign aboard a U-boat. *LB*

The insignia of U-103 commanded by Viktor Schütze was the victory rune. It was adopted by all the U-boats in the 2nd Flotilla after the summer of 1941. *LB*

The insignia of Jürgen Oesten's U-106 was a sawfish. *LB*

## EARTHENWARE TILES WITH THE INSIGNIA OF LORIENT U-BOATS

The insignia of the German war shipyard in Lorient. *LB*

The insignia of U-108 under Commander Klaus Scholtz was the blazon of Danzig, its patron city, and the polar bear following its first patrol off the south of Iceland. *LB*

The insignia of U-123 was chosen by Commander Karl-Heinz Moehle after his U-boat had been seriously damaged when a ship rammed it when it was 14m underwater. It represents the Wound Badges awarded to soldiers. *LB*

The insignia of U-128 was the same as the *Todt Organization* which was based in Pont Callac Chateau, and which had "adopted" this U-boat. *LB*

The insignia of U-107 was four aces because Commander Günther Hessler was one of the U-boat "Aces." *LB*

The insignia of U-109 is the German ex-servicemen's organization "*Kyffhäuserbund,*" founded in 1900, and which sponsored this U-boat. *LB*

The insignia of U-124 was an Edelweiss. It was chosen by Commander Georg-Wilhelm Schulz following help given by the *Chasseurs Alpins* to the crew of his first U-boat that had been sunk off Norway. *LB*

The insignia of U-129 was a lion with the motto "*Westward-ho*" over it; this motto was also on U-37, and was added by its former commander, Nicolai Clausen. *LB*

# SOUVENIRS OF GÜNTHER PRIEN'S U-47

Snakes and ladders game called "Prien against England." *LB*

A board game based on Scapa Flow Port. *LB*

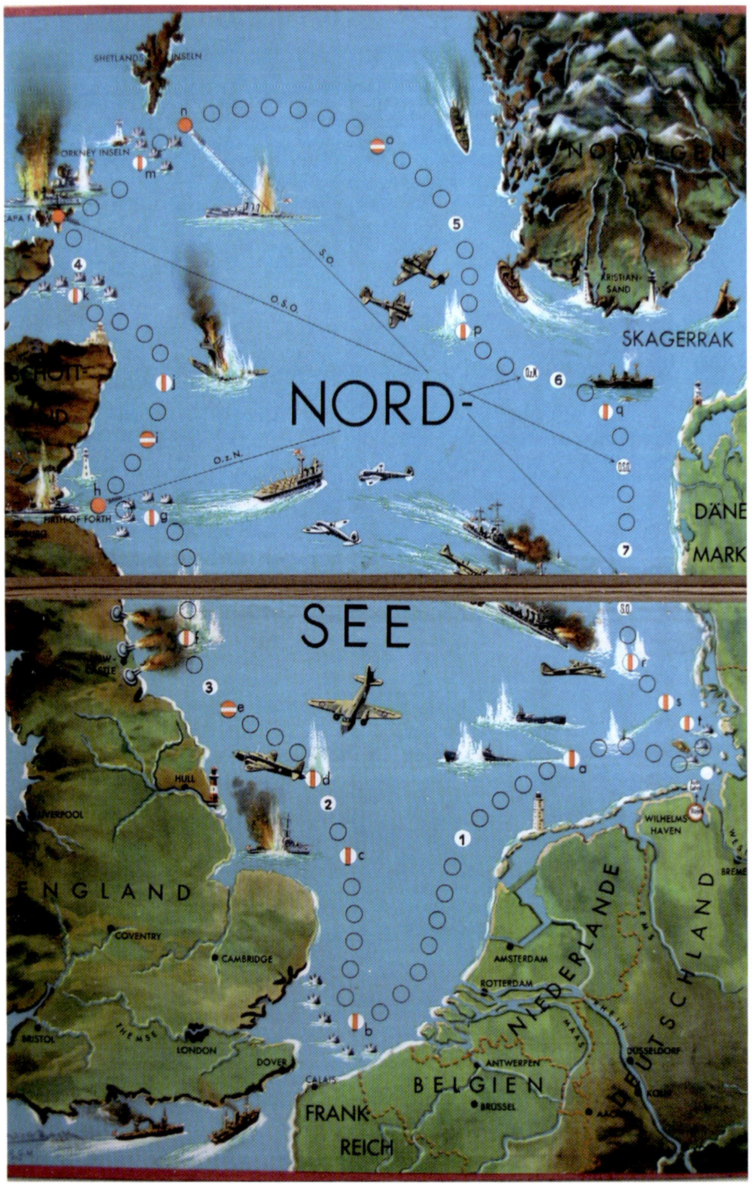


Game of snakes and ladders: landing on the square Scapa Flow allowed the player to advance twenty-seven squares! *LB*

China plate with U-47 on it. *LB*

A postcard signed by Prien. If he had returned from his patrol aboard U-47, he would have been given the command of U-501. *LB*

Cover of a small booklet sold by school children to German citizens with Prien on the cover. The profit went to the Winter Aid for the soldiers. *LB*

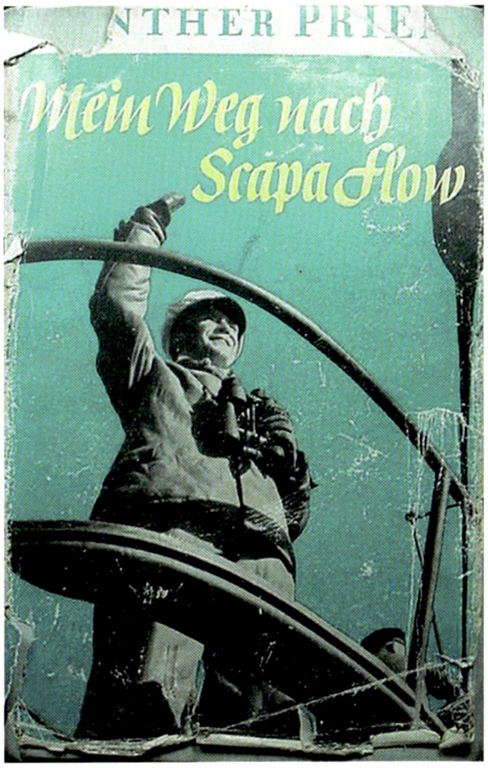


Günther Prien's book about his special patrol in Scapa Flow in October 1939. He had been granted special leave to give him time to write it. *LB*

A very rare color photo of Prien arriving in Lorient on October 23, 1940, which appeared in the German magazine *Signal* in January 1941. *LB*

"*Chez Mélanie,*" the retaurant in Riec-sur-Belon, where Prien and his officers liked to eat before leaving on patrols. Today the building houses the Tourist Office. *Benoît Senne*

## PLAQUES AT THE SUBMARINERS MÉMORIAL, MÖLTENORT

This color photo of Joachim Schepke appeared in the April 1941 edition of *Signal* magazine, although he had already been lost at sea. He offers a scale model of a U-boat to the son of the skier Tony Plenk, with whom he had lodged during his stay in Ruhpolding ski resort in Bavaria in January 1941. *LB*

The Memorial of the Submariners of Möltenort was inaugurated on June 8, 1930. It lists the names of the submariners killed during the First World War. *LB*

The gray leather jacket belonging to Otto Kretschmer was given to the U-Boot-Archiv in Cuxhaven. *LB*

Plaque recording the exact number of German submariners killed between 1939 and 1945: 30,000 out of a total 39,000 enlisted: 77% of losses. *LB*

The plaque with the names of those who died aboard U-32. The commander's name always appears, even if he did not die at sea. *LB*

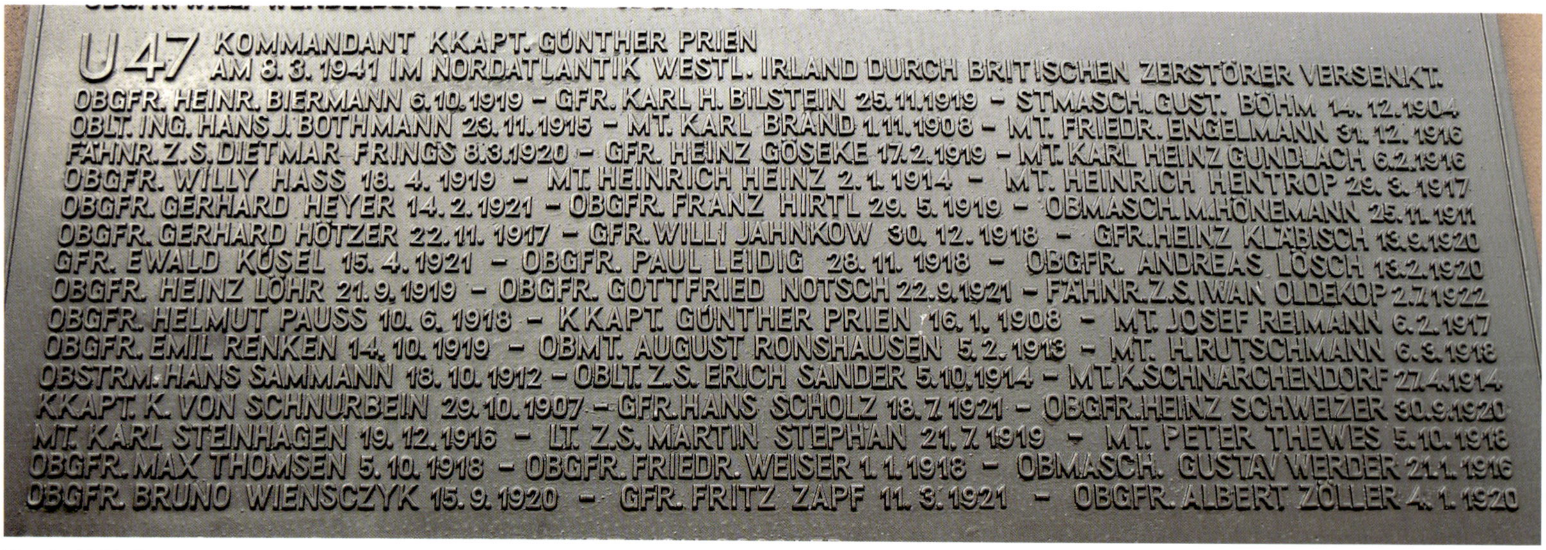


Plaques for each of the U-boats sunk. The plaque with the names of the crewmembers aboard U-47 lost at sea. *LB*

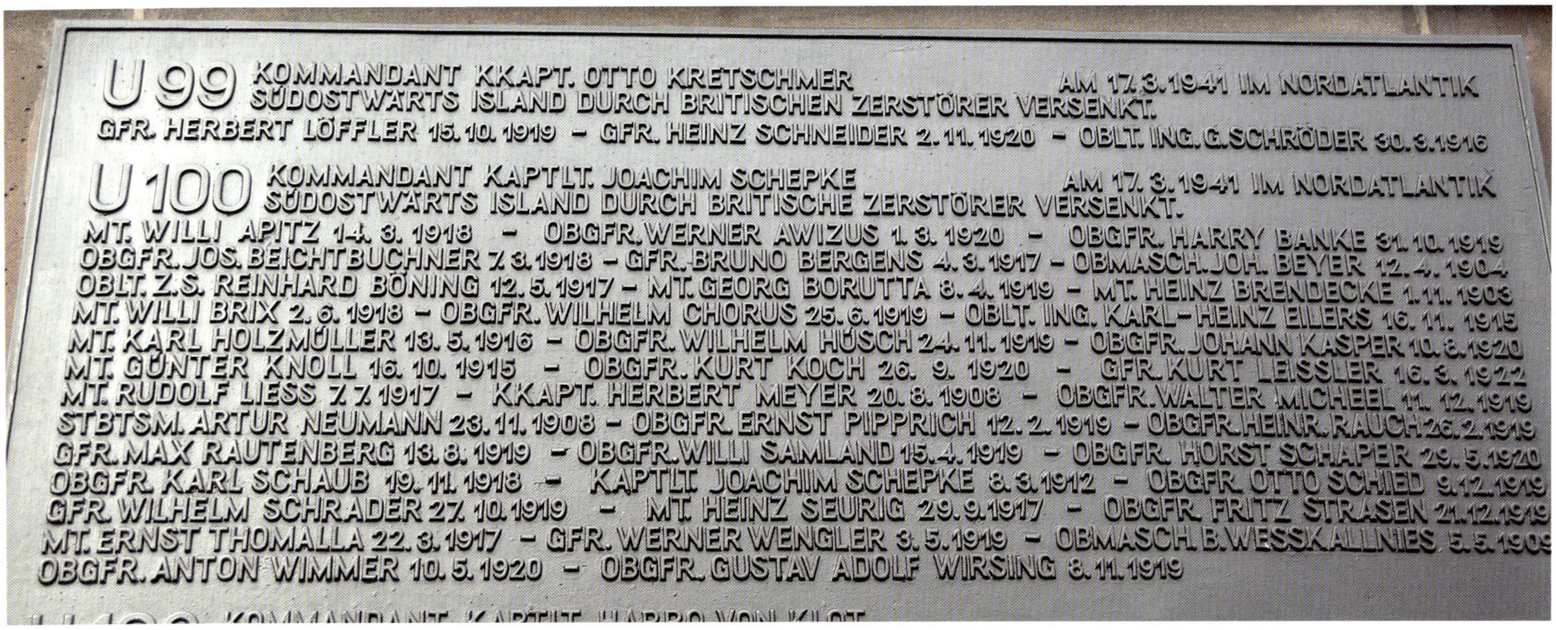


The names of those lost aboard U-99 and U-100. *LB*

The plaque of U-110. *LB*

The Finnish submarine *Vesikko* was a prototype of the first German II-type U-boats; it is also the only example to have survived the war. Turned into a museum in 1959, it can be visited on a small island in Helsinki Port, Finland. *Sébastien Hervouet*

U-35, U-boat of the 2nd Flotilla, is on the cover of the American magazine *Life* in October 1939! *LB*